RotoVision

Innovation in Book Design

Charlotte Rivers

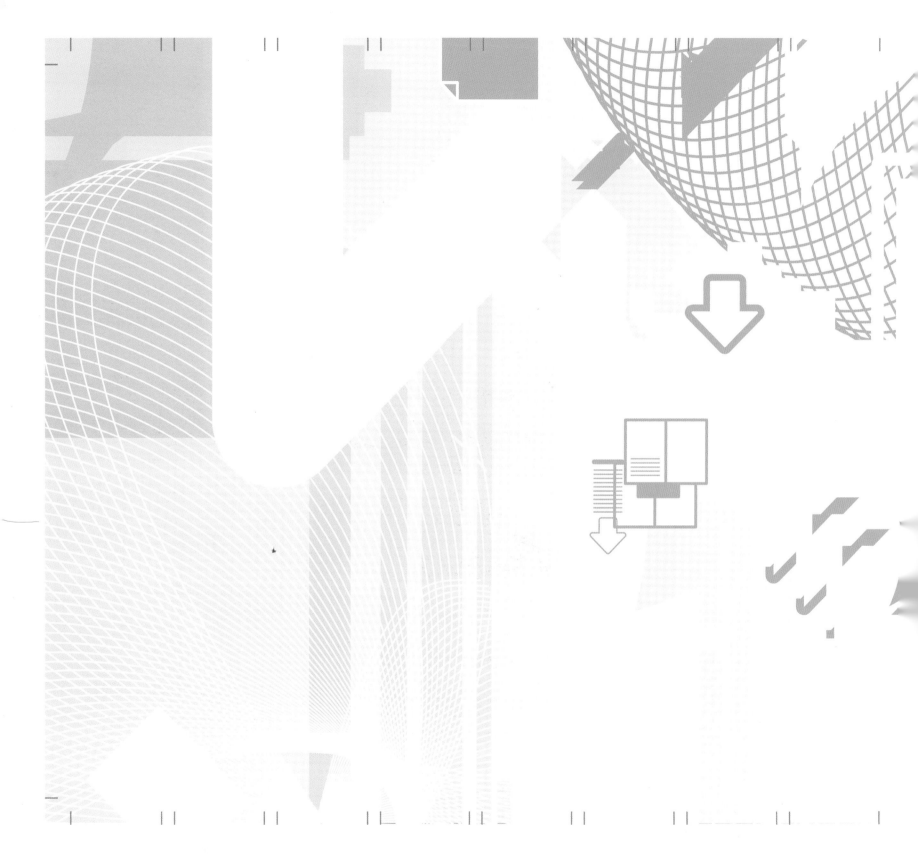

# book-art

Innovation in Book Design

Charlotte Rivers

A RotoVision Book

Published and distributed by RotoVision SA
Route Suisse 9
CH-1295 Mies
Switzerland

RotoVision SA
Sales and Editorial Office
Sheridan House, 114 Western Road
Hove BN3 1DD, UK

Tel: +44 (0)1273 72 72 68
Fax: +44 (0)1273 72 72 69
www.rotovision.com

10 9 8 7 6 5 4 3 2 1
ISBN: 978-2-940361-69-4

Art Director: Jane Waterhouse
Design: Simon Slater, www.laki139.com
Photography: Simon Punter

Reprographics in Singapore by ProVision Pte. Ltd.
Tel: +65 6334 7720
Fax: +65 6334 7721

Printed in China by Midas Printing International Ltd.

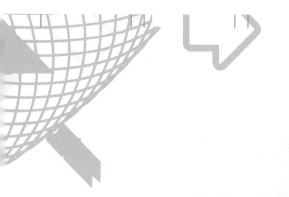

# Contents

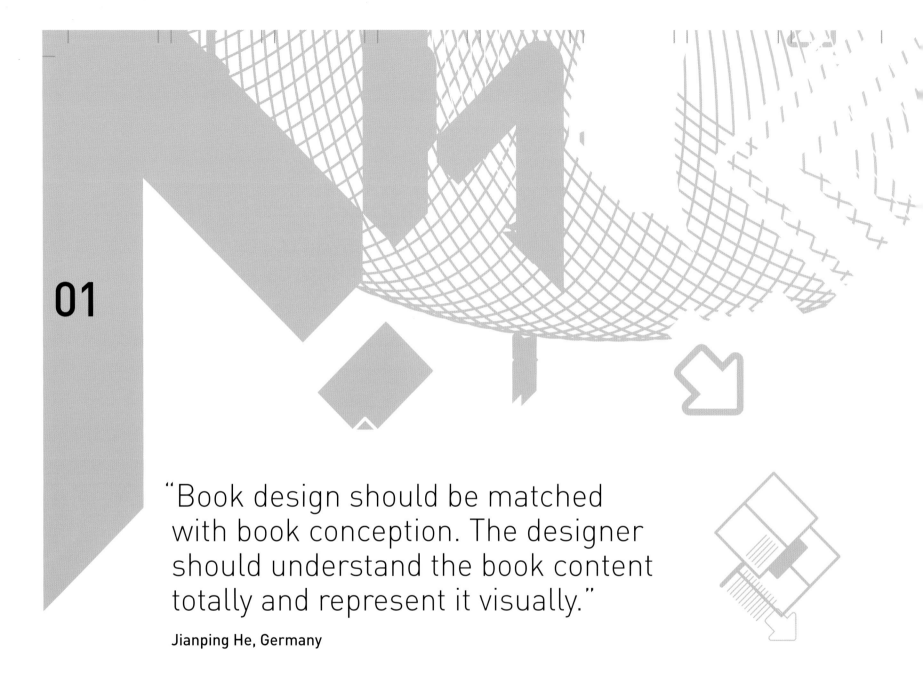

**01**

"Book design should be matched with book conception. The designer should understand the book content totally and represent it visually."

Jianping He, Germany

# Introduction

For a time it was widely believed that we would see the demise of the book, given the fact that so much information was being made available on the Internet. But in fact, quite the opposite has happened. Book sales have continued to rise year on year and the format has become a much-loved and much-needed antidote to our increasingly technology-driven world. This makes sense. For many of us, much of our time is spent looking at screens—computers, televisions, iPods, cell phones—so there is something particularly refreshing about picking up a book and reading it, or simply leafing through its pages. On top of this, book publishing has become home to some of the most interesting and innovative graphic design work seen today, a global selection of which is showcased throughout this book.

As with magazine publishing, it tends to be the smaller, independent publishers, and those who choose to self-publish, who are producing this work. Much of the best of such work is designed by creatives, for creatives. Look at the shelves of a specialist art and design bookstore and you'll find them packed with showcase-style books and designer monographs. Some of the better-known examples include Bruce Mau's collaboration with Rem Koolhaus to produce S,M,L,XL; Aboud Sodano's book for fashion designer Paul Smith, You Can Find Inspiration in Everything*; and Irma Boom's book Sheila Hicks: Weaving as Metaphor.

However, great design is also to be found in fictional titles from mainstream publishers. Faber & Faber republished its Poetry Essentials series in a box set, with each title displaying a beautiful typographic cover. As Darren Wall explains, "When I started at Faber, one of my first aims was to get designers to do work for us that was just as groundbreaking and beautiful

as the work they do for music and advertising clients. It always seems like publishing design lags behind other industries in terms of innovative work, and I was keen to do something that made people sit up and take notice, to challenge people's expectations of what a book cover could be," he adds.

Then there is My Penguin, a series of six Penguin classics, republished in 2006, including Virginia Woolf's The Waves and Jane Austen's Emma. The books come with blank covers, inviting the reader to create their own design, and upload it to an online gallery. In 2004 Penguin published Great Ideas, a collection of political and philosophical polemics designed by David Pearson. On a tight budget, he managed to create a series of covers that went on to win a number of design awards.

It is difficult to put a date on the birth of editorial design, but it was revolutionized in the mid-fifteenth century when movable type was invented and the first substantial book—the Gutenberg Bible—was published. Since then it has evolved radically. Publishing landmarks include the arrival of Jan Tschichold at Penguin in 1947. He transformed the publishing house and set the bar for modern book design. Other significant publishing/design partnerships include New York–based Zone Books and designer Bruce Mau, and, of course, "the closet thing to a rock star in graphic design today" (USA Today), Chip Kidd and New York publishers Knopf.

Another significant influence on editorial design is the continuing improvement in production values, which means there are an ever-increasing number of ways in which designers can differentiate their book. Faced with decisions such as which paper stock to use, what ink to print with, which typeface to select, whether to emboss the title on the cover …

the designer must make careful, considered choices.
As Jon Dowling of SEA Design explains, "Design is about choice and the success or failure of a piece is dependent upon whether we, as designers, make those choices in an informed and sympathetic manner. From the stock and typeface to the imagery and finishing of the book, all should echo the essence of the subject matter, without interfering with or commandeering the piece. A good book cover is firstly one that stands out from the others on the shelf, and secondly one that tells its audience exactly what it is."

So, should we judge a book by its cover? This is a matter of opinion. In one sense it is expected that the viewer should judge a book by its cover because, with design standards so high, why shouldn't they see the presence, or lack of good design as an indicator of the quality of the book's content. As Jim Stoddart at Penguin explains, "A piece of writing deserves to be read on its own merits, but a book is a complete object that people interact with and keep, and how it looks and feels is a big part of that." This point also made by designer Vince Frost. "Good book design is where the designer does justice to the content. It's like going into a beautiful restaurant and having terrible food. It needs to be great in all ways."

However, as designer Nick Bell points out, "Too many good books are let down by poor covers." While this is true, I think that many of us can't help but judge a book by its cover, especially those of us who hate bad design as much as we love good design.

Through Book-Art, I aim to showcase a collection of innovative book designs that challenge the norm and give the reader something extra. Fiction or nonfiction, all the books included have one thing in common—they are unique and memorable objects of desire. As consumers become more and more design conscious, so the designer has to meet their demands. As the examples on the following pages show, in this endeavor they are succeeding.

**Charlotte Rivers**

## 02

"A good book cover is like an honest smile and a firm handshake."

Joe Marianek, USA

# Covers & Packaging

"A good cover is one that strikes a balance between presenting the experience of the book and capturing a particular vision or essence."

Brett Phillips, Australia

# Introduction

The cover and packaging of a book are the first things that any potential reader sees, and the role of both in grabbing the attention of that potential buyer is vital. Although mainstream book publishing still uses quite standard design—book title, author name, and an image—there are plenty of smaller, independent book publishers who are pushing the boundaries when it comes to cover and packaging design. This chapter looks at prime examples of this, from the use of bellybands and slipcases to unusual binding techniques, and innovative use of imagery.

Design: **Paul Reardon**
Art Direction: **Peter and Paul**
Illustration: **Kid Acne**
Publisher: **Robert Horne Group**
Country: **UK**

## Kid Acne

To promote paper supplier Robert Horne's colored Kaskad stock, design practice Peter and Paul created this book together with graffiti artist, rapper, and illustrator Kid Acne.

"Our decision to work with Kid Acne (aka Edna) and produce a book about his work was in direct response to placing the papers in a modern context," explains Reardon. "Edna's work is very prevalent at the moment, but our decision was also about complementing the paper. Edna uses flat, muted earthy colors and often in a limited palette, which works well over the neutral-colored papers in the range.

"We wanted to do a lot of mixing and matching of colors, which made it a challenge to get it working harmoniously," he adds. "We used French folds so that we could have more control over where we placed colors, and we also used shortfall pages for the interview sections in order to get strips of color next to each other. In addition, we developed an intricate wraparound that interlocks two sheets of different tints."

The book features a wide selection of Kid Acne's existing work alongside specially commissioned artwork, unique to this project. Its grid system enables the layout of images to flow from page to page in one continuous stream.

Design: **Melanie Mues at Mues Design**
Photography: **Stephen Gill**
Publisher: **Nobody Books**
Country: **UK**

## Buried

Buried features a collection of photos by Stephen Gill that were buried by the photographer, near where they were taken. Mues used this as her inspiration for the design of the book, and buried each copy before retrieving and presenting them in a clean, blind-embossed slipcase. The result is that each book has different degrees of smudging and deterioration on the cover.

"My relationship with this client has been shaped over the many projects we have done together," explains Mues. "Stephen is very aware of design that overpowers the content, so his brief was to find a format, material, and treatment for the book that reflected the playful, hands-on approach of this particular project."

As well as the slipcase, each book (only 750 were printed) comes with a print from the photographic series.

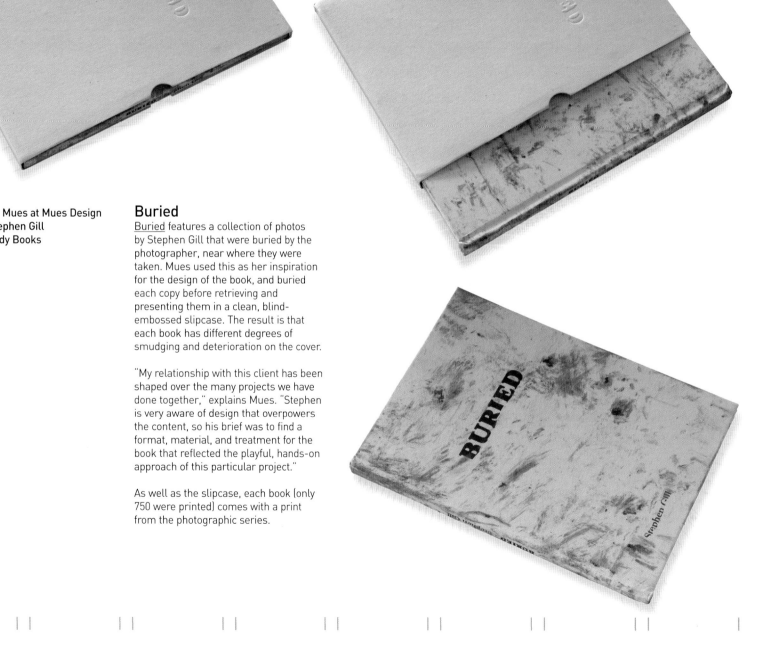

Design: **Jianping He**
Art Direction: **Jianping He**
Publisher: **Hesign Publishing**
Countries: **Germany/China**

## AGI: New Voice

Up until 2004, the AGI (Alliance Graphique Internationale) produced regular annual reports, but for its 2004/2005 edition it decided that a more substantial book, featuring the work of new AGI members, should be produced together with reports about the AGI Congresses in Beijing (2004) and Berlin (2005).

"The brief was totally open apart from the size of the book and the title, AGI: New Voice," explains He. "When I found out the title I immediately imagined an ear hearing this 'new voice,' so I tried to design a book with an ear. We also focused all the layout and cover design on the word 'voice;' loud on the inside, but with a calm cover featuring an ear."

The headline typeface is Corel Standard, with OCR A 13T used throughout on Menken massive ivory stock. As the cover has an ear on the bind, it proved difficult to find a binding technique that would work. Therefore an old traditional Chinese binding method was used. Instead of being glued, the pages have been punched and then bound with yarn.

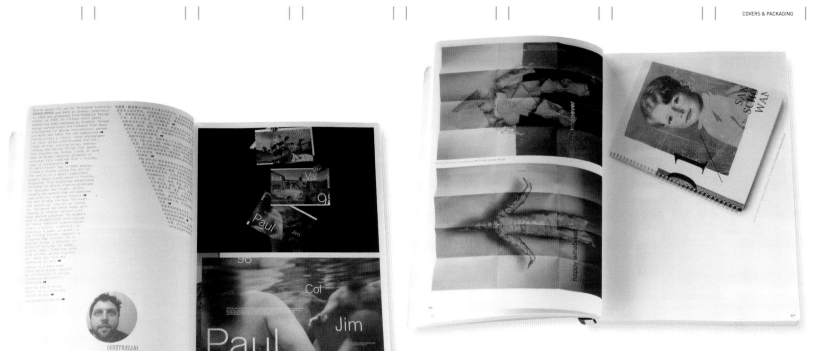

### ANDREW ASHTON

(AUSTRALIA)
安德鲁·阿什顿（澳大利亚）

### MARKUS DRESSEN

(GERMANY)

Design: **Jianping He**
Art Direction: **Jianping He**
Publisher: **Hesign Publishing**
Countries: **Germany/China**

## All Men Are Brothers

All Men Are Brothers is a self-commissioned project that features interviews and the work of 108 leading contemporary graphic designers. "The title is the name of a Chinese classic novel, which tells the legend of 108 Robin Hoods during the times of Zhao Zhen, Emperor Renzong of the Song Dynasty (1010–1063 AD)," explains He. "What these 108 people try their best to establish is an ideal nation, a Utopian kingdom. We thought the 108 heroes and our 108 designers had something in common: the designers intend to set up an ideal kingdom of graphic design."

An illustration of each Robin Hood has been matched to one of the 108 graphic designers. The book is presented in a hard slipcase that has been wrapped with traditional Chinese paper and die cut with three holes in the forms "1," "0," and "8." The color stripes on the pages are visible through the "0."

ITC Officina Sans Book typeface was used throughout, printed on 120gsm Antalis paper for the inner pages and 220gsm Conqueror Laid Black for the cover.

Design: **WE RECOMMEND**
Art Direction: **WE RECOMMEND**
Publisher: **Plan 8**
Country: **Sweden**

## Attityd/Miljö/Planering

Malmö-based Plan 8 is a consultancy for environmental planning. These three books describe its core competencies: Attitude, Environment, and Planning (attityd, miljö, and planering).

A hardback gray cloth cover has been used for all three books, with different-colored bellybands (red, green, and brown, respectively) used to distinguish one from the other.

Because of the nature of the content within the books, the design has been kept minimal and functional. A standard two-column grid has been used in which to set the text and other content. Arial was used inside the book and Chalet—for its clean and modern feel—on the covers.

Design: **Lotta Kühlhorn**
Art Direction: **Lotta Kühlhorn**
Publisher: **Rabén & Sjögren**
Country: **Sweden**

## Majas Morsas Kompis Sambo

Majas Morsas Kompis Sambo (Maja's Mum's Friend's Cohabitee) is a book of short stories aimed at young people. "I wanted to make an image that looked like this author's language," explains Kühlhorn, "as though the girl in the stories had printed the text on the cover in her own way."

Kühlhorn selected text from the novel and handwrote it in a circle. It reads, "An upper secondary school. A couple of breakdowns. A few love stories. A handful of treacheries. Much fear. Even more longing. Eleven short stories."

The typeface has been applied to the cover with offset printing and blind-print glossy enamel.

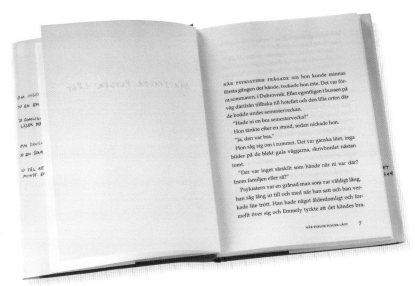

Design: **Katja Hartung at Sopp Collective**
Art Direction: **Katja Hartung**
Photography: **Martin Mischkulnig**
Publisher: **Self-published**
Country: **Australia**

## Martin Mischkulnig

This book features the work of Martin Mischkulnig, whose photography falls into four categories: people, places, advertising, and projects. These categories were used to structure the book into four separate booklets, housed within a slipcase.

"Since the photography has to be so prominent, all other design elements were kept very minimal," explains Hartung. "The use of special packaging and production finishes adds another layer of quality to the contents that complements rather than overwhelms."

The booklets, printed offset, were bound with a simple saddle stitch. The cover of each booklet repeats the first internal shot in the form of clear foil (white on white), with a slight deboss effect. The slipcase is covered with buckram paper and includes Martin Mischkulnig's name as a deboss. Attached to the inside of the slipcase is a black ribbon: pulling this draws the booklets out. Garamond typeface has been used throughout.

Design: **Bob Aufuldish**
Art Direction: **Bob Aufuldish**
Publisher: **The University of Denver,
    Victoria H. Myhren Gallery**
Country: **USA**

## In Limbo

<u>In Limbo</u> was created to accompany
a class in curatorial practice at the
University of Denver, and an exhibition
of the same name. Contemporary art
collectors Vicki and Kent Logan made
their collection available to the class.
The students then viewed the collection,
developed a theme, wrote essays, and
assembled the exhibition under the
direction of a faculty advisor.

The design of the book was inspired by
the exhibition theme. "I was struck by the
transient psychological states the art
expressed," explains Aufuldish, "and
I arrived at the idea of trying to express
in-between and indeterminate qualities
typographically." He selected Eidetic
Sans and Eidetic Neo as they are
indeterminate in their style—neither
serif nor sans serif.

The cover boards are trimmed flush with
the book block, and the essay typography
runs flush to a frame that appears and
disappears throughout the book. The
cover has an interesting feature, with
the title stamped in a clear foil.

Design: **Sarah Noellenheidt and Matthias Ernstberger at Sagmeister Inc.**
Art Direction: **Stefan Sagmeister**
Production: **Lara Fieldbinder/ Melissa Secundino**
Publisher: **Guggenheim Museum, New York**
Country: **USA**

## The Hugo Boss Prize 2004

This book was published to celebrate the occasion of the Hugo Boss prize in New York. Each of the finalists created their own spreads, and Sagmeister Inc. created the book's cover. Text was applied to the cover using laser cutting and mirror foil.

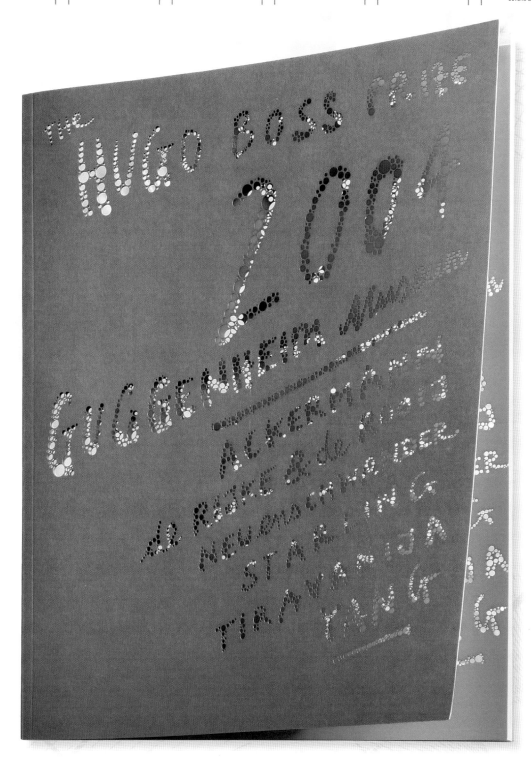

Design: **Giorgio De Mitri at Sartoria**
      **Comunicazione**
Art Direction: **Sartoria Comunicazione**
Photography: **Geoffroy de Boismenu**
Publisher: **Damiani Editore**
Country: **Italy**

## The Conversation

The Conversation, limited to a run of 200, was created to accompany an exhibition held in Paris by de Boismenu. Many different materials have been used on book covers—this displays one of the more unusual: slate. It was created by gluing two 1 x 1in (25 x 25mm) slate slabs onto cardboard flyleaves, which, in turn, were glued to a Cialux spine. The spine is fixed with metal rivets.

The concept behind it is "organic." "There is no other way to describe it," explains De Mitri. "The first way the book communicates to the reader is through the sense of touch. The slate cover conveys the idea of 'organic' in a better and more straightforward way than any word could."

Between these two slabs of solid stone lie a series of images, laid out simply, but beautifully, one image to a page, making it very much a statement book.

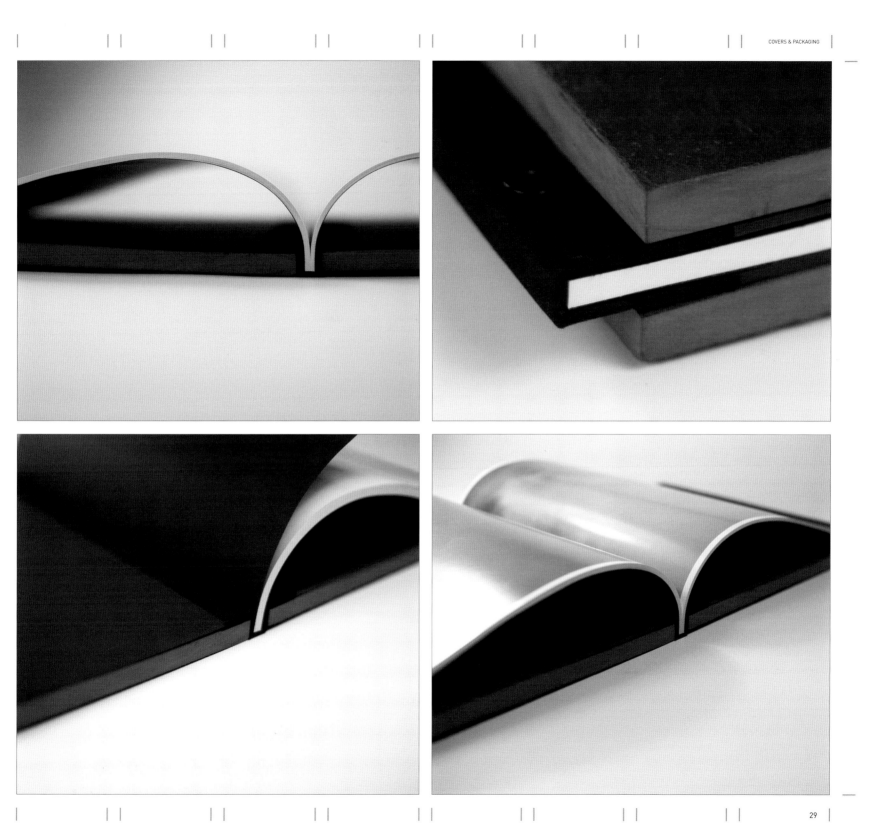

Design: **Bob Aufuldish**
Art Direction: **Bob Aufuldish**
Photography: **Kevin Hester**
Publisher: **Denver Art Museum**
Country: **USA**

## RADAR

This book accompanied the opening of an exhibition of the same name at the Anschutz Gallery, part of the Denver Art Museum (DAM).

"I was especially pleased and fortunate to work directly with the curatorial team at DAM on this," explains Aufuldish. "It meant they were able to articulate their thinking behind calling the exhibition RADAR, which was that the Logans have a unique ability to find interesting contemporary art before it hits the wider art market.

"This led to many of the ideas I used in the design, from the macro choice of cover image (is that the Mona Lisa or not?) to the micro choice of typefaces," he adds. "I often build a project out from the typeface selections, and in this case it was especially interesting to try to use type subtly to reinforce the ideas behind RADAR."

The main cover image is Monna Lisa in its Origin by Yasumasa Morimura. However, the text on the slipcase obscures the face of the subject so, for a moment, it could almost be mistaken for the Mona Lisa.

The primary typeface is Retina by Tobias Frere-Jones. Adobe Janson has been used for italics, with any text in quotation marks set in Avenir.

Design: **Mark Diaper at Eggers + Diaper**
Art Direction: **Mark Diaper**
Publisher: **Laconic/The Whitstable Biennale 2006**
Country: **Germany**

## Lost

Lost is unusual in that it is an art project in its own right. The book lists key things that the artist, Simon Faithfull, has lost during his lifetime (his virginity, his parents, cell phones, sunglasses, etc.), each time relating the story of the object's "departure." During the 2006 Whitstable Biennale, copies of Lost were left in restaurants, on buses, on the beach, lying on the street, and in various pubs. Those who found them were encouraged to fill in their name and where they had found the book, then asked to "lose" it in another public place for someone else to find. A website ran in conjunction with the project, and the notes on this reveal that the books are slowly spreading across the world—one is currently in New Zealand. The brown paper cover gives it the feel of a package; this works perfectly with the concept of the book as a traveling art project.

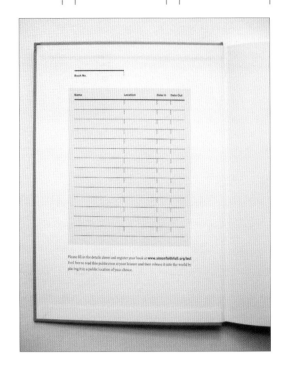

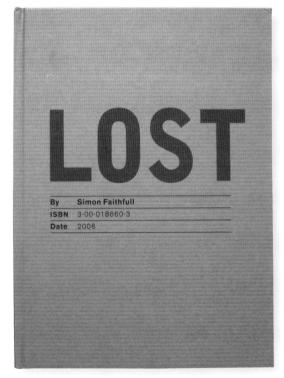

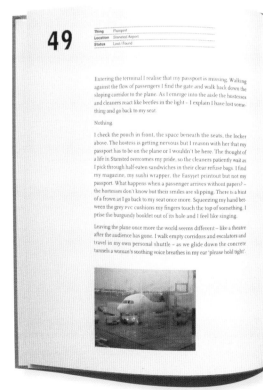

Design: **Angus Hyland at Pentagram**
Art Direction: **Pentagram**
Publisher: **Canongate Books Ltd.**
Country: **UK**

## Under the Skin

Under the Skin is a beautifully written tale that introduces Isserley, a woman obsessed with picking up hitchhikers, as long as they are male, muscular, and alone. Why hitchhikers? As the novel unfolds and the reason is made explicit, the reader is drawn inexorably into a completely unexpected and increasingly terrifying world.

The cover design presents the reader with a visual (and tangible) reference to the story and title of Michel Faber's novel. The cover of the paperback visually suggests something under the skin; the flesh-colored translucent jacket reveals an image of a dark and eerie road, peeling off into the distance.

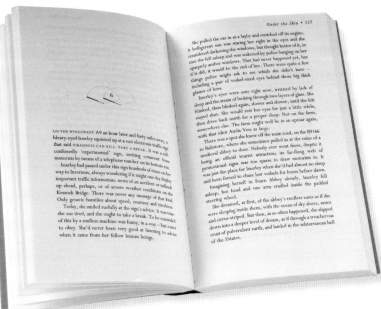

Design: **Sam Borkson and**
**Arturo Sandoval at FriendsWithYou**
Art Direction: **Robert Klanten**
Editors: **Robert Klanten/Hendrik Hellige**
Publisher: **Die Gestalten Verlag**
Countries: **Germany/USA**

## Friends With You Have Powers!

Friends With You Have Powers! is a monograph from FriendsWithYou's Borkson and Sandoval, who combine classical disciplines that fuse art, illustration, and toy making. It displays a comprehensive collection of their work across various media from graphic design, painting (fine art), toys, character design, videos, interactive installations, and hotel room designs.

"The challenge was to create an interesting and entertaining way to show the scope of their work in the different media formats," explains Klanten. "We decided on a padded book cover, and through this we tried to reveal the inner quality of the work. The padded cover provides a soft, tactile experience similar to the plush toys they design and create."

The cover features FriendsWithYou's most representative character, Malfi. The typeface used, T-Star, is the Die Gestalten Verlag house font.

Design: **Matthias Ernstberger
and Roy Rub at Sagmeister Inc.**
Art Direction: **Stefan Sagmeister**
Photography: **Ed Burtinsky**
Editor: **Alex Steffen**
Publisher: **Harry N. Abrams, Inc.**
Country: **USA**

## Worldchanging

Worldchanging reports new, positive developments in science, engineering, architecture, business, and politics that will change the world. The brief was to design a book that would appeal to a large audience, not just people who were already concerned about green issues.

"We wanted the book to look and feel authoritative, like a definitive guide for all bright green solutions for the twenty-first century," explains Sagmeister. "At the same time, it needed to be pretty enough to leave out on a coffee table, without being a coffee-table book."

Over time the book cover (100-percent recycled paper) will become significantly yellowed by the sun shining through the die-cut holes of the slipcase. As the book is a compendium, the designers adhered to a tight grid, allowing for easy scanning of the various contents.

Design: **Angus Hyland at Pentagram**
Art Direction: **Angus Hyland**
Publisher: **Canongate Books Ltd.**
Country: **UK**

## The Fahrenheit Twins

This is Michel Faber's second collection of short stories. The cover illustrates the title story—a tale of androgynous twins living in the Arctic. Two silhouettes found in a book of 1980s Japanese trademarks and logotypes formed the basis of the design. Though their origin is unclear, the silhouettes replicated an Edwardian style of illustration, echoing the story's overall modern-fairy-tale feel. Faber had a very clear idea of what the twins should look like and sent a photograph, which had been the inspiration for the story, to Hyland. It was an image of two Sami

children in folk costume from an old issue of National Geographic magazine. Through discussions between Faber and Hyland, the twins evolved from their original, traditional form into the final offbeat renderings, complete with pointy hats and furry boots.

The silhouette was applied to the cover using black foil block. The book is bound as an unsewn hardback with a round back, a four-color (CMYK) printed paper cover, head- and tailbands, and one-color, patterned endpapers.

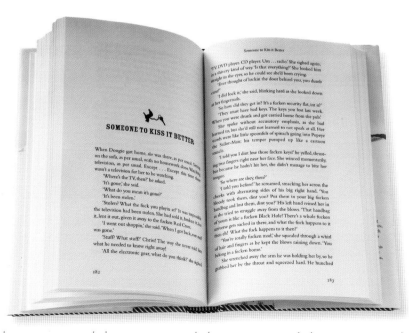

Design: **Atsuki Kikuchi**
Publisher: **Verlag für Moderne Kunst**
Countries: **Japan/Germany**

## Takehito Koganezawa: Drawing

Takehito Koganezawa: Drawing focuses on Koganezawa's drawings rather than the video and performance works for which he is best known. Kikuchi worked closely with him in selecting and ordering the drawings for inclusion in the book. "Since the artworks are the subject matter of the book, the main design work was to place them right and change their size and position on the page," explains Kikuchi. "The overall concept was to keep all additional information in the book as minimal as possible and let the artworks speak for themselves."

A two-column grid was used for the text pages and a three-column grid for the list of plates. The textured cover has an image embossed on the front and text embossed on the spine. The book is bilingual, with English set in Helvetica and Japanese set in Chu-Gothic.

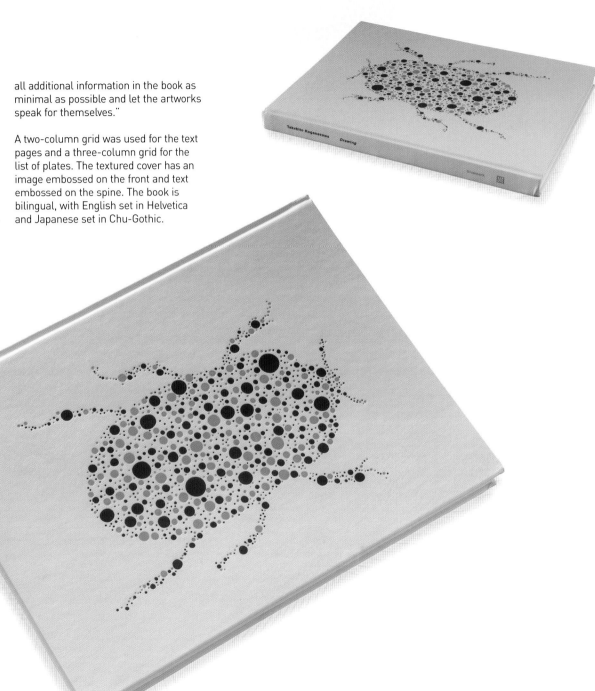

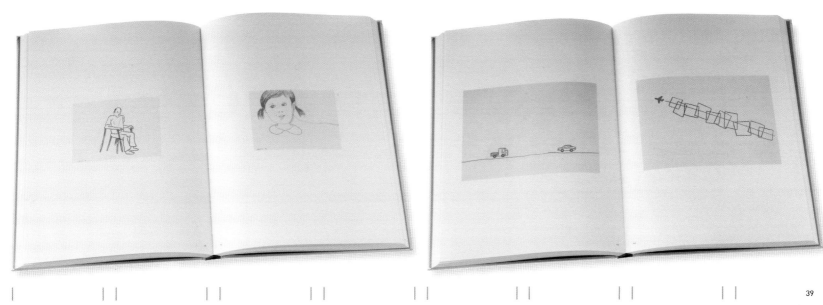

Design: **Nick Bell and Matt Willey**
    **at Nick Bell Design**
Art Direction: **Nick Bell**
Photography: **Martin Parr**
Publisher: **Chris Boot**
Country: **UK**

## Mexico

This coffee-table-style book displays Martin Parr's photographs of Mexico. The brief was to present them in a distinctive and durable format.

"Inspiration came from the content and from Martin Parr's past work," explains Bell. "Parr's work exposes our questionable taste and in doing so celebrates it. Our primary aim was to reject all existing graphic-design formalism (the canon of taste), with the objective of producing a book in questionable taste. Something unapologetically garish and blunt," he adds. "So we did a tour of shops selling tacky printed stickers with glitzy finishes in order to loosen our inhibitions."

Rather than select one image to represent the book's content, the cover simply features the word "Mexico." A radiating pattern of rays and Martin Parr's name in repeat was impact printed onto prismatic foil, and "Mexico" screen printed over the top of this, in two colors. The book is perfect bound, with separate blockboard front and back covers glued to the endpapers that form the spine. A special edition was also produced, with a box sleeve containing a Parr print in a paper envelope on the inside cover.

# MARTIN PARR MEXICO

Design: **William Hall/Nicholas Barba**
Photography: **Adam Reich**
Publisher: **Xavier Hufkens Gallery**
Countries: **UK/Belgium**

## Robert Ryman

This book was created to accompany
an exhibition by painter Robert Ryman
at the Xavier Hufkens Gallery in Brussels.
As one of the founders of the Minimalist
movement, Ryman's paintings are
exercises in control and reduction.
Invariably using a square format and
white paint, he sensitively explores
brushwork, surfaces, and materials.

"Such a refined collection of work
required a delicate response which
allowed the paintings visual space,"
explains Hall. "Each work is isolated
on its own page, and in order to unify
the images, all background color was
carefully replaced with the same muted
neutral tone."

The cover features the artist's surname
on linen material, which relates to the
bare canvas often left exposed in his
work. His surname is printed on the front
cover, and his first name on the back.

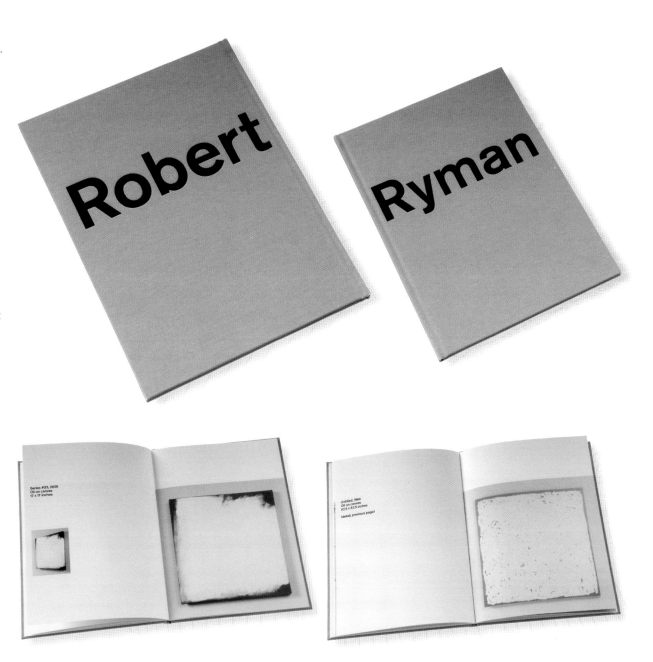

Design: **Deanne Cheuk**
Art Direction: **Deanne Cheuk**
Illustration: **Deanne Cheuk**
Publisher: **:B Publishing**
Country: **USA**

## Mushroom Girls Virus

Mushroom Girls Virus is a self-published
collection of 12 months' work by New
York–based Cheuk, revolving around the
theme of girls and mushrooms. Cheuk's
psychedelic drawings, paintings, and
illustrations show her inspiration, from
mushrooms and dreams to art nouveau.
She fuses meticulous pencil drawings
and collages of girls, landscapes,
mushrooms, and birds, with sporadic
bursts of watercolor and 3-D elements
of mushrooms and graphic shapes.

The book cover is made with linen cloth
and fully embroidered using gold thread.
"I designed the cover in this way because
I wanted a cover that was tactile and
precious, almost like a family heirloom,"
explains Cheuk. The book also has
a gatefold poster insert.

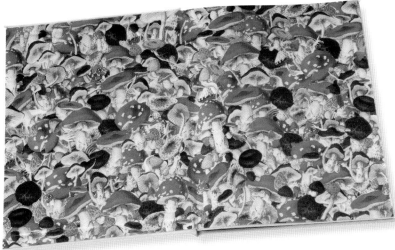

Design: **Nicolas Bourquin/Sabrina Grill**
Art Direction: **Robert Klanten**
Editors: **Robert Klanten/**
    **Nicolas Bourquin/Claudia Mareis**
Publisher: **Die Gestalten Verlag**
Countries: **Germany/Switzerland**

## Altitude

Altitude presents and examines current
trends in Swiss graphic design. The book
showcases flourishing contemporary
designers. It gives insight into the impact,
essence, and diversity of their work and
evaluates the significant evolution of
Swiss illustration and typography.

The design reflects the dynamic content
of the book. The packaging and cover were
inspired by both the Swiss landscape and
graphic design. The cloth on the cover,
the embossing, and the special binding
all give the book a tactile, well-crafted
look and feel that is characteristic of
Swiss design.

Joël Tettamanti's photograph Untitled,
from the series Cols Alpines, was used
on the cover. LaPolice was used for the
body typeface and Gravur Condensed for
the display typeface.

The book has an open-spine binding.
A sheet of linen was attached to the first
and last pages, and a slipcase was added
for extra protection.

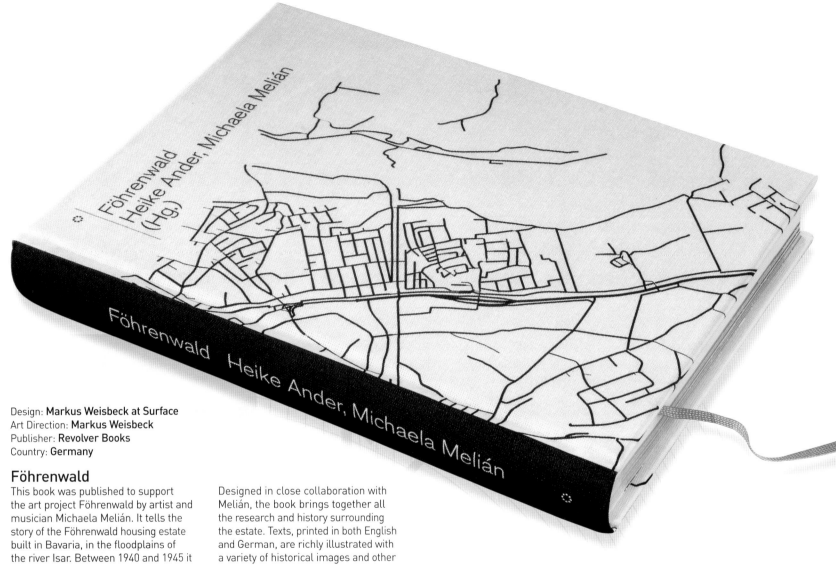

Design: **Markus Weisbeck at Surface**
Art Direction: **Markus Weisbeck**
Publisher: **Revolver Books**
Country: **Germany**

## Föhrenwald

This book was published to support the art project Föhrenwald by artist and musician Michaela Melián. It tells the story of the Föhrenwald housing estate built in Bavaria, in the floodplains of the river Isar. Between 1940 and 1945 it served as a camp for workers from Nazi munitions factories, after World War II it became a transit camp for displaced Jews, and from 1955 voluntary occupants, mainly displaced families from eastern Germany, moved to the estate.

Designed in close collaboration with Melián, the book brings together all the research and history surrounding the estate. Texts, printed in both English and German, are richly illustrated with a variety of historical images and other material. The imagery on the linen cover—an abstract map of the estate in 2007—corresponds with the historical maps on the first three spreads. The book is printed in black and white, with all texts set in Univers 45 and 55.

## Brett Phillips, 3 Deep Design, Australia

**What and when was the first book you designed?**
I think that Bird (2002) was perhaps one of the first books we commissioned, designed, edited, and published that had real merit. In the context of independent Australian cultural publishing, it was a benchmark project that charted new ground for us in terms of consideration and resolve. It also challenged the conventional role of the artist's book. With 2,500 copies, 17,500 embroideries, 200 pages, five different stocks, handmade case and covers, and two years in development, it was definitely one of most challenging and ambitious projects we have yet undertaken.

**When approaching book design, what inspires you?**
Above all, content! It should really be the starting and finishing point for a designer. It should provide the initial framework for conceptual development and one of the last points of reference and critique. We find that content is the key to uncovering possibilities and opportunities in any project. As part of the design process, and working beyond an initial concept, there will no doubt be many points of inspiration—historical reference, cultural influences, personal collections, one's own individual design sensibility ... All of these things will help shape the final design outcome, but I think that the content—the proposition, the essence—should really drive any initial response.

**What makes a good book cover?**
A good cover is one that strikes a balance between presenting the experience of the book, without having to spell things out, and one that captures a particular vision, essence, or position. It is also about being subtle, refined, and knowing what one doesn't have to say to make it work. I think that the best covers are those that seduce the viewer.

**How much of a role do you think the designer plays as a marketer in the retail environment?**
Well, I think that if you removed all of the marketing managers from the process, the creative world, and retail spaces, would be much more interesting and textured places. It is quite simple. Great designers are great thinkers. They have the ability to resolve complex spatial problems regardless of media, and it seems as though the more complicated and layered marketing managers make the process, the more people forget that this is the case.

**What are the best and worst things about designing books?**
The best thing: the experience of getting it right and the smell of freshly printed ink on handmade Italian paper. The worst thing: marketing managers.

**How would you design a book if there were no limit to budget?**
The same way we design every other book—with consideration to content, form, and experience. The challenge for any designer is to propose the best of a circumstance regardless of budget, timing, content, and/or client. We have made the most of every budget (big and small), but if there were no limit to budget we would probably produce a beautiful, single-color document, and I would be writing this in the sun from the south of Italy!

**Do you judge a book by its cover?**
Of course. I think that the experience of a book is the same as life—everyone wants to be seduced.

## Jianping He, Hesign, Germany

**What and when was the first book you designed?**
In 2001 I designed and edited <u>Before 30</u> (Hentrich & Hentrich, Germany) which featured a collection of work that I completed before I was 30.

**When approaching book design, what inspires you?**
Mostly, the ideas for book design come through understanding the book's contents, and sometimes new printing techniques and new materials give me inspiration.

**What makes a good book cover?**
I think that the reduction of a book's contents and simple binding always make a good book cover.

**How much of a role do you think the designer plays as a marketer in the retail environment?**
The most important thing here is the conception of the book, I think. Book design should be matched with book conception, so the designer should understand the book content totally and represent it visually with his or her design idea. Therefore, I think the designer has 49-percent importance as a marketer in the retail environment.

**What's the best thing about designing a book?**
The best thing about designing a book is when experimental book design ideas are accepted by clients.

**Do you judge a book by its cover?**
No, though I think the conception and content behind the book cover are important.

# 03

"Books are 3-D posters for themselves."

Joe Marianek, USA

Artwork

"I believe it to be much more engaging for the reader when a design merely hints at the book's contents and allows them to fill in the blanks."

David Pearson, UK

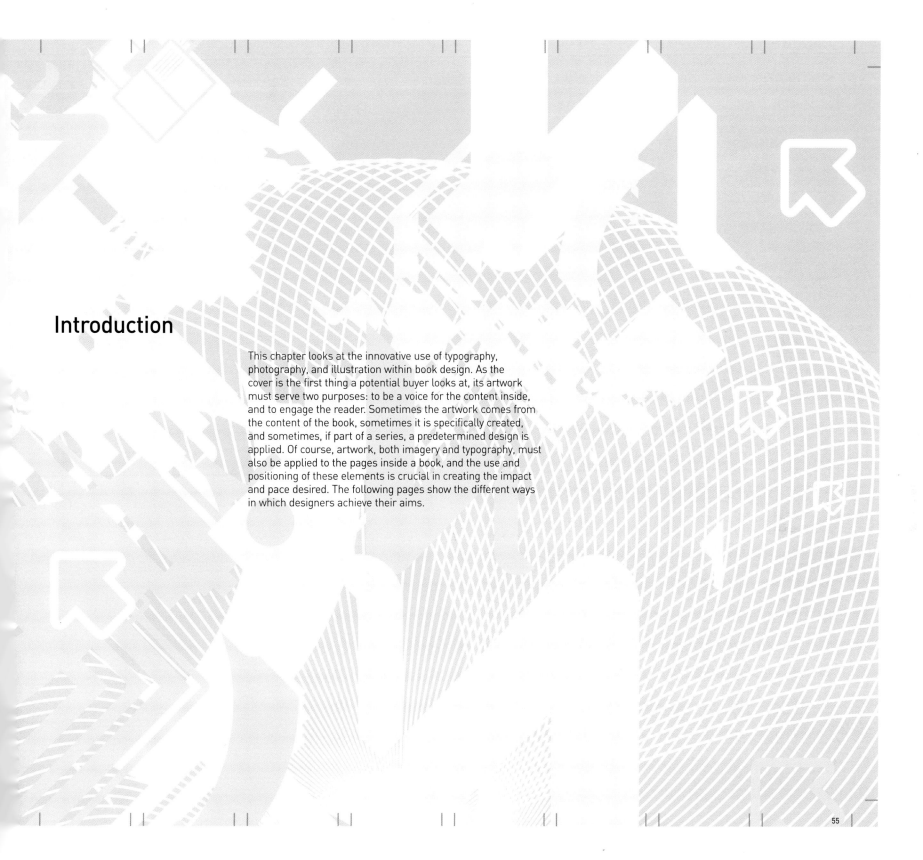

# Introduction

This chapter looks at the innovative use of typography, photography, and illustration within book design. As the cover is the first thing a potential buyer looks at, its artwork must serve two purposes: to be a voice for the content inside, and to engage the reader. Sometimes the artwork comes from the content of the book, sometimes it is specifically created, and sometimes, if part of a series, a predetermined design is applied. Of course, artwork, both imagery and typography, must also be applied to the pages inside a book, and the use and positioning of these elements is crucial in creating the impact and pace desired. The following pages show the different ways in which designers achieve their aims.

Design: **Jan Wilker and Hjalti Karlsson**
**at karlssonwilker inc., with**
**Frank De Rose**
Art Direction: **Jan Wilker/Hjalti Karlsson**
Publishers: **FIA Art Group/Publikum**
Countries: **USA/Serbia**

## karlssonwilker's
## 12 Days in Serbia

karlssonwilker's 12 Days in Serbia is
part of a wider project that the New York–
based designers embarked upon in 2004.
Hjalti Karlsson and Jan Wilker went to
Serbia for 12 days to explore Serbian
design and culture, then offered their
views, interpretations, and findings to
a Serbian and international audience.
Most importantly, each day they created
one piece of work influenced by what they
heard, saw, experienced, and ate, resulting
in a "real-time design" adventure.

The outcome of the trip is not only this
book, which features behind-the-scenes
information and interviews, but also a
calendar, website, TV documentary, and
exhibition. The book is bilingual: English
and Serbian. To save space, the designers
ran both languages together, setting one
in red and the other in blue, with almost
no leading. For legibility, readers are
provided with a vellum sheet on which
white stripes are printed. These block out
every other line when placed over a page.

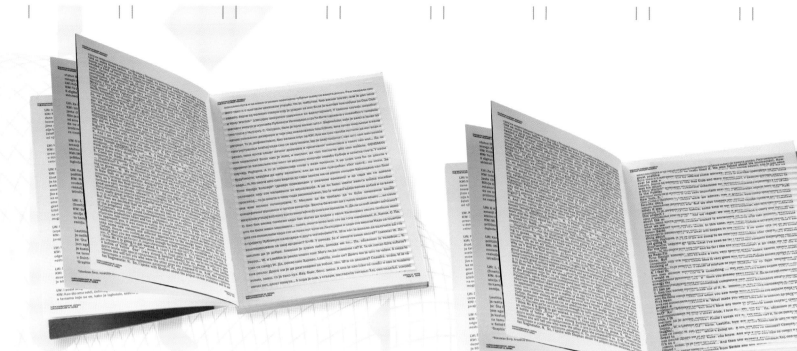

Design: **Frost Design**
Art Direction: **Vince Frost/**
   **Anthony Donovan**
Photography: **Vince Frost**
Publisher: **Frost Design**
Country: **Australia**

## Frost* (sorry trees)

Frost* (sorry trees) was published to coincide with Frost's exhibition at the Sydney Opera House in early 2006. Its aim was to show where ideas come from and how they are realized through the design process. It features case studies of a wide range of projects undertaken by Frost, including magazine and book design, stamp design, exhibitions, corporate literature, signage, etc.

Each project is shown against a backdrop of Vince Frost's own photography, creating an extra layer that turns up the volume so the book acts as a design piece in its own right. A loose grid was used within the book, allowing for more flexible design. It was printed on 100-percent recycled bulky newsprint to give it a scrapbook feel.

## Fourth Estate

Book publisher's catalogues (Fourth Estate) London, 1996-2004

When it came to the design of its catalogues, Fourth Estate was always prepared to think outside of the box. Rather than producing a standard catalogue, this young, independent publisher would approach different designers to come up with a different visual theme for each one. The brief for these projects rarely extended beyond a list of book titles, as the covers had yet to be designed. This meant devising a concept for the catalogue, as well as coming up with innovative ways to represent the books featured within. Between 1996 and 2004, Frost designed six Fourth Estate catalogues in a range of sizes and formats, each one surprising and entertaining its audience in new ways. These included a traditionally produced letterpress catalogue, a screenprinted catalogue, a set of playing cards, a set of paper swatches and a catalogue created using carbon duplicate paper.

"I love creating type, bit type is no more physical than digital"

"while rummaging around the printers I found this tray of discard
metal type which I think is great example of accidental typography"

## Super Cheap Auto

Annual Report (Super Cheap Auto) Sydney, 2004-2005

As its name suggests, Super Cheap Auto isn't a company lacking in confidence, a point reinforced by the bold, brash design of its identity and packaging. So, rather than trying to create a 'designed' annual report Frost, along with Ray Parslow, partner at Frost Design, decided to embrace the company's bold aesthetic instead, using its own visual vernacular to really have fun with the design and create a unique report that looked like it was produced by the staff themselves. The main visual elements were key words featured on products and packaging around the store, which were photographed and then featured throughout the report. For example, the logo for the store's battery and electrical range, Super Force, was photographed and juxtaposed with an image of its staff. The company logo – a dollar sign – became the opener to the financial section, which was printed on receipt paper, and the cover was based on the 'redback' shocking used in all Super Cheap Auto stores. The final report, packaged in typical Super Cheap Auto packaging, went on to receive numerous awards and has seen designers from around the world calling the company to request copies!

**35**

"a wall of bagged annual reports were hung at the company's agm"

library – a relaxed environment but also a productive one." It was the right approach and before long he found himself looking for new assistants to share both the workload and the 12ft long table around which they would all sit. During this time, Frost was asked to design a commemorative set of stamps celebrating fifty years of the British National Health Service, a commission that came about as a direct result of his work on the Independent Magazine. "Contrary in approach, the stamps were not too dissimilar; both have to tell a complex story within a single frame." For Frost, knowing that millions of these stamps would be created was a thrill in itself; that the smallest design he had ever created – in physical terms was the largest, in terms of its number. Early ideas for the project included a set of 'intelligent' stamps that could provide nutritional information! For example, a stamp that, when licked, would indicate on the front whether you were getting enough vitamin C. A year after setting up the Clerkenwell studio, Frost was surprised to receive a call from Condé Nast, publishers of Vogue magazine. A subsequent meeting at Vogue House in London's Hanover Square revealed that the company were planning to launch two new titles – Russian Vogue and Japanese Vogue, or Vogue Nippon. Frost was offered the position of Art Director on Vogue Nippon, swiftly followed by a trip to New York to meet the editor of American Vogue, Anna Wintour, and spend a week in the US Vogue office learning "how things were done." "I remember thinking, this is it; this could be my major breakthrough, but at the same time thinking, why me?" he recalls. "There was a feeling that something wasn't quite right but I was so thrilled by the opportunity I didn't stop to think any further than that." Having long been an admirer of Italian Vogue's art direction and photography, the opportunity to be part of this world was incredibly exciting. Frost was also a huge fan of both the late Alexey Brodovich, and Fabien Baron, former Art Director of both Italian Vogue and Interview and Creative Director of Harper's Bazaar.

By January 1999, having enlisted friend and designer, Derek Samuel, to run the London studio, Frost was on a plane to Tokyo along with Sonia and their six-month old son, Luca. Arriving in a new city was never going to be easy but nothing could have prepared the Frosts for what lay ahead. Japan was like a completely different world and, unable to either speak or understand the language, even the simplest of tasks caused problems. "The first time I took a cab I went to open the back door and the driver started shouting and yelling because they have electric doors and you're not supposed to touch them – and then, when he finally let me in I couldn't even tell him where I wanted to go!" The Vogue office had already been set up in Tokyo but with no design department in place it was up to Frost to find everything from design assistants to computers – and then get the whole system up and running. Moreover, now that the magazine had its Art Director the pressures were on to produce a dummy of the magazine. All Frost had, however, were questions – and very few answers. Would there be any English in the magazine? How would the type work? Was the grid

my little bundle of love, gbs, 2006

different to Western grids? What about Japanese fonts? The questions just kept on coming. Playing with words and type had always been integral to Frost's approach, yet here he was working in a foreign language with no idea what he was even laying out. "I'd be sitting in this huge boardroom with editors and advertisers, all nodding politely and having lengthy conversations in Japanese and I couldn't understand a damn thing – except that 'yes' usually meant 'no'!" he recalls. "Any project I work on, it's all about listening to the client, looking for clues but when you can't understand them there is no emotion, no clues, nothing." While Tokyo's heated toilet seats went down a treat, the earthquakes and tremors did not and Frost would regularly find himself on all fours under the desk as the building shook to its core. Faced with one daunting task after another, the pressure soon began to take its toll. Unable to attend any meetings without a translator, and working with a Japanese editor who all but refused to acknowledge his existence and a French deputy editor whose response to everything was a flat, "no, no, no, we don't do it like set 'ere", putting together a design team was virtually impossible. Offering more money proved fruitless with Tokyo's loyal design community, as did talking to other magazine art directors. In desperation he even tried trawling the local art colleges for work placement students, but only succeeded in attracting a tortured free art student, armed with a very squeaky trolley loaded with paintings, who thought the job would be "so unbearable it would help me with my art!" He left the building somewhat quicker than he had arrived. Trying to familiarise himself with Japanese photographers was equally problematic. As Frost quickly discovered, albeit a little late, in Japan you didn't call a photographer's book until you had decided to work with them. "All of a sudden we had about a hundred photographers all thinking they were working for Vogue who had to be told they weren't!" Amidst the chaos in Tokyo, Frost was also overseeing the output from his own studio in London and would spend most nights on the phone to the UK liaising with one or more of the five designers he had working there. Although email was now commonplace, broadband was not, which meant sending and viewing images was still a lengthy process. But working such long hours came at a cost – Frost saw very little of his family. While he headed off to work at the studio each day, Sonia was left to fend for herself in a strange city where she knew no one and understood nothing. Not much fun for a new mother with a young child. The final straw came one evening as he headed home in a cab, pumping away at the stress ball he had bought to try and alleviate the strain – until it exploded all over the floor. Arriving at Frost's apartment the driver, oblivious to what had occurred, turned round to see his passenger looking incredibly frustrated and with his fist – at which point he leapt out of the car shouting and screaming, fists raised ready to defend himself! Frost did succeed in designing and producing a dummy issue of Vogue Nippon but after eight months in Tokyo and several cancelled launches for the magazine, he was eventually released from his contract.

Design: **Melanie Mues at Mues Design**
Art Direction: **Alan Fletcher**
Publisher: **Phaidon/Richard Schlagman**
Editor: **Craig Garrett**
Country: **UK**

## Contemporary Artists series

Phaidon's Contemporary Artists series focuses on the work of iconic sculptors, painters, photographers, and other artists. "The challenge was to come up with the right ingredients to communicate the authority of this series—featuring high-profile authors and editors—as well as getting across its contemporary content," explains Mues. "The books had to look neutral enough to stage the different personalities of the artists, but still breathe the soul of each individual. The design also had to withstand time; Phaidon wants it to last 10 years."

Her redesign for the series features a full-bleed image by the artist together with the artist's and author's names in large type in a text box on the cover and spine. A high-gloss UV varnish was used to emphasize these text boxes. This was a conscious step to promote the A-list authors commissioned for each book.

Mues chose a combination of two typefaces—Foundry Gridnik and Minion—to reflect the contemporary and academic character of the series.

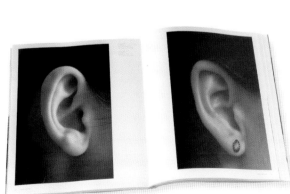

Design: **Birna Geirfinnsdóttir/Hörður
Lárusson/Sól Hrafnsdóttir**
Publisher: **Commercial College
of Iceland**
Country: **Iceland**

## V71

<u>V</u> is an annual for the student body
at the Commercial College of Iceland.
The theme for this edition was the
100th anniversary of the school. Much
of the content and material featured is
produced by students of the college.
The idea behind the design was that
the content should not be outshone
by the graphics. The image on the
cover is a remake of that used on the
very first issue of the annual. "<u>V71</u> is
the seventy-first issue, and throughout
the years the covers have changed.
We decided to go back to the beginning
because of the theme of the paper,"
explains Lárusson.

Spot varnish features on all 237 pages,
used on photographs and graphics.
The book is bound with a three-part
binding and flush trim, and comes
packaged in its own plastic carry case.
This is finished with an image of a suit,
positioned to "clothe" the statuesque
figure on the front cover.

Design: **Various**
Art Direction: **Darren Wall at Faber Design**
Publisher: **Faber & Faber**
Country: **UK**

## Poetry Essentials

This Faber & Faber box set is a collection of the best of the publisher's famous poetry list. "We wanted this series to be accessible to as many different people as possible—young and old, academic and casual readers—and even to appeal to people who may not ordinarily buy poetry," explains Wall. "My intention was to commission designers not normally associated with book design and get them all to work together to produce one beautiful collection."

Wall commissioned several designers to create the typographic covers: Making Cocoa For Kingsley Amis was designed by Kerr | Noble; Kid was designed by Kam Tang; Ariel by Darren Wall; Crow by Build; The Waste Land by Sanderson Bob; High Windows by Sam Renwick at This is Real Art; Death of a Naturalist by Gradiate; Tell Me The Truth About Love by Parra at Big Active; Old Possum's Book of Practical Cats by George Wu; and The War Poems by Harriman Steel.

Each designer was asked to produce a two-color, typographic response to the poetry. "Everybody responded in a different way. Kerr | Noble decided to represent the domestic tone of Wendy Cope with typography made from a smashed mug," explains Wall, "and Kam Tang produced a solution built from symbolic images mentioned in Simon Armitage's text. I wanted everyone's response to be very different while still part of a recognizable set; the aim was for each cover to be capable of standing alone as well as be part of a set."

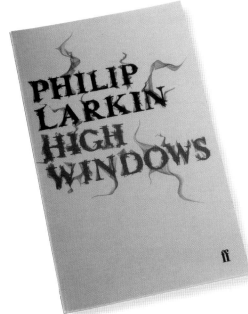

Design: **Gerard Saint**
Art Direction (cover): **Gerard Saint/**
  **Mat Maitland**
Photography (cover): **Patrick Ibanez**
Publisher: **Die Gestalten Verlag**
Country: **UK**

## Head, Heart & Hips

Head, Heart & Hips: The Seductive World of Big Active plays with the universal themes of seduction and pleasure. It features specially commissioned work not only by the Big Active design studio, but also its associated artists, including Jasper Goodall, René Habermacher and Jannis Tsipoulanis, Kate Gibb, and Will Sweeney.

The cover features an erotic depiction of the Big Active "Boy & Girl" motif set among a garden of giant lilies. It pays homage to Prince's 1988 Lovesexy album cover, which Saint felt set an appropriately grand visual tone for the book. The title is printed as a clear spot UV varnish. The book also features a silk-ribbon marker cut to resemble a serpent's tongue.

Design: **Melanie Mues at Mues Design**
Art Direction: **Melanie Mues**
Publisher: **Tate Publishing**
Country: **UK**

## Looking Back, Thinking Ahead

Looking Back, Thinking Ahead reviews and celebrates five years of the Tate Gallery's Continuing Professional Development (CPD) program for teachers. It showcases the philosophy of the Tate Education Department with the help of diagrams and projects successfully undertaken between 2000 and 2005.

The brief was to present clear, structured academic content in an interesting and creative way. "It is very unusual to showcase education work in a book," explains Mues. "It is academic and, as a result, quite dry subject matter."

To overcome this, Mues has broken the content down into small chunks and interlaced them with full-bleed images. The cover features details of a large spider diagram explaining the structure of the program. Mues has used parts of this diagram on the individual divider pages of the related chapters. Further hand-drawn diagrams feature throughout in a light and digestible manner.

The book is enclosed in a gift box. Foil blocking in gloss pink on rough Dutch grayboard gives it a tactile and modern feel. Mues has used the Tate font as per the corporate identity guidelines, with outline versions for the headlines.

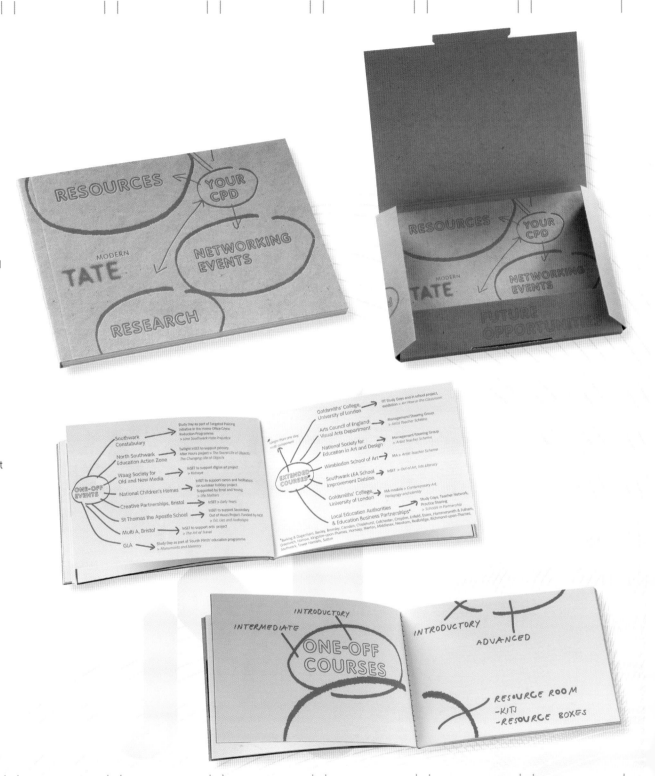

Design: **Spin**
Art Direction: **Spin**
Publisher: **Cultureshock Media**
Country: **UK**

## Owning Art

Owning Art is intended for people with
an interest in, or involved with buying,
contemporary art. The design brief was
to create an accessible typographic guide
with a sophisticated feel—classic, with
a contemporary twist. To this end the
decision was made not to use any imagery,
but instead to make a feature of the
quotes in the book. These have been set
in ITC Cooper Light; the body and display
typeface is Akkurat Regular and Bold,
and the caption typeface Akkurat Mono.

The book is casebound and section-sewn.
Two-color foil blocking was used to apply
text to the front and back cover, which is
gray Wicotex Brillianta binding cloth.

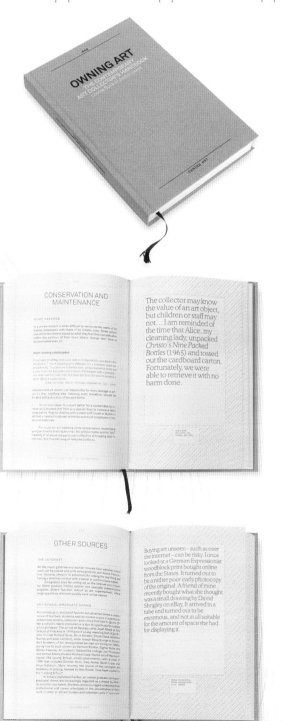

Ellery

Design: **Jonathan Ellery at Browns**
Art Direction: **Browns**
Publisher: **Ellery/Browns**
Country: **UK**

## 87

A conceptual piece forming part of Ellery's one-man show held in early 2007, <u>87</u> looks at numbers, form, pace, and rhythm.

"The book takes numbers at face value, dispensing with their utilitarian nature and celebrating instead their visual form," explains Ellery. "The numbers are in sequence with nothing else on the page, each spread becoming an artwork in its own right."

With <u>87</u> Ellery has followed the tradition of artists such as Martin Kippenberger, Ed Ruscha, and Lawrence Weiner, who have all produced conceptual art books. "This is a conceptual piece. The book itself is the defining art piece," adds Ellery. "It is an act of typographic curatorship on my part, but it is not a book specifically about the type; it's more about a concept and ambiguity regarding its existence in the first place."

The book was printed in a limited run of 2,000, with the first 200 housed in a slipcase. It was thread-sewn in 12 sections and has a semirigid, hardback cover that is covered with cloth and printed with matte-black foil, as is the slipcase. Ellery used Univers typeface on the cover and 87 different typefaces through the book.

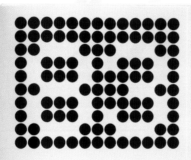

Eighty Seven
Jonathan Ellery ©

First Published July 2006
Ellery/Browns ©

Browns
The Flag Store
29 Queen Elizabeth Street
London SE1 2LP
England
www.brownsdesign.com

Design: **Undoboy**
Art Direction: **Undoboy**
Illustration: **Undoboy**
Publisher: **Rhett Austell**
Country: **USA**

## Man and Space

Shown here is a redesign of the 1960s Time-Life book, <u>Man and Space</u>. The book looks at the history of man and space, in particular the various technological developments that have allowed its exploration. This version uses two grid systems on each page: one for the text and another for the illustrations.

Clean and classic serif Garamond has been used for body text and captions, with modern-look Bauhaus for the titles. This fits well with the instructional illustrations that were inspired by early 1960s record-cover designs.

Bold colors were used to separate the different sections of the book. These were chosen to represent the colors that run from the earth to the universe—red as the core, green as grass, yellow and orange as mountains and rocks, and blue as the atmosphere. Undoboy wrapped the book cover in silver material stuffed with cotton wool to make it feel soft.

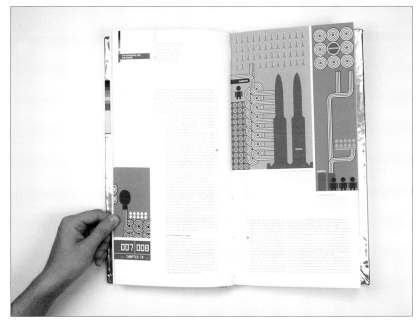

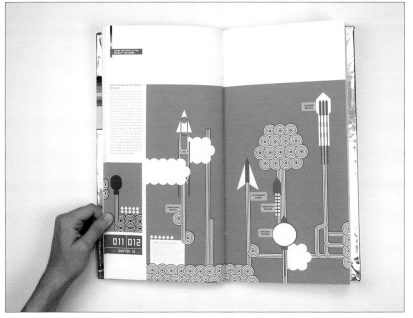

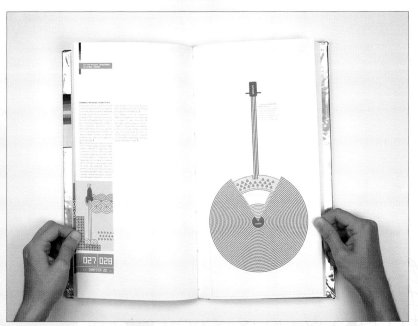

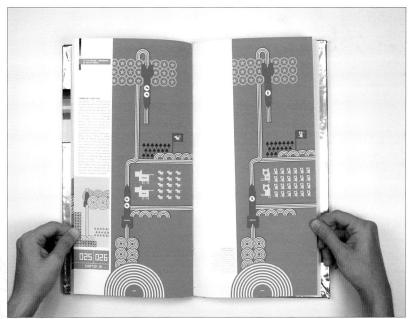

Design: **Frost Design**
Art Direction: **Frost Design**
Photography: **Anthony Geernaert**
Publishers: **Object: Australian Centre for Craft and Design/Melbourne Museum**
Country: **Australia**

## Freestyle

Freestyle was produced to accompany an exhibition of the same name, about contemporary Australian design. The brief was to create a book that effectively presented the works of 40 designers, and was a design statement in itself. It was also vital to incorporate the branding of sponsors Bombay Sapphire.

To do this, the designers used a blue transparent Perspex square, referencing the sponsor's blue glass bottle, as a framing device for the artists and their work. Each designer was photographed in their own environment, interacting with the blue frame in their own way.

The square form was carried through to the Freestyle identity, which uses a modular geometric typeface. The squares were also used as the structural grid for the book, website, and other items.

## Adam Goodrum

What is design?
What is creativity?

Whether you design a building
or a watch or a chair, it is an
act of creativity. A fashion
designer can create a building ...
People have the potential to
do anything, if they are creative ...
Design can change a city or
move a culture ... and Australian
design is world class.

Marc Newson

design is my way of life

design is a col...

design is not

getting your hands dirty

design is...

STARTING A NEW SENTENCE

## Dinosaur Designs

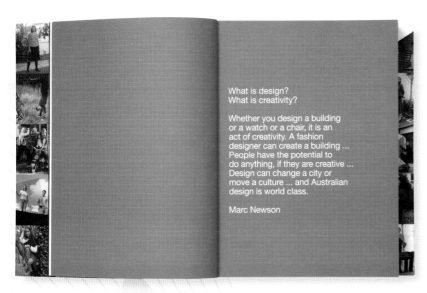

Design: **SEA**
Art Direction: **SEA**
Photography: **Rankin**
Publisher: **SEA**
Country: **UK**

## Extraordinary Friendships Through Breast Cancer

<u>Extraordinary Friendships Through Breast Cancer</u> aims to raise awareness of the importance of women having sufficient support to cope with the illness. Containing advice and relating personal experiences, it explores the friendships of celebrities who have been touched by breast cancer. These testimonials are complemented with portraits by Rankin.

"The idea of photographing celebrities and the friends with whom they have shared a breast-cancer experience is to highlight the fact that breast cancer is a frightening disease that touches everyone. The intimacy of the photography reflects the closeness of the friendships," explains Palmer.

The positioning and styling of the typography throughout the testimonials reflects the theme of conversations between friends.

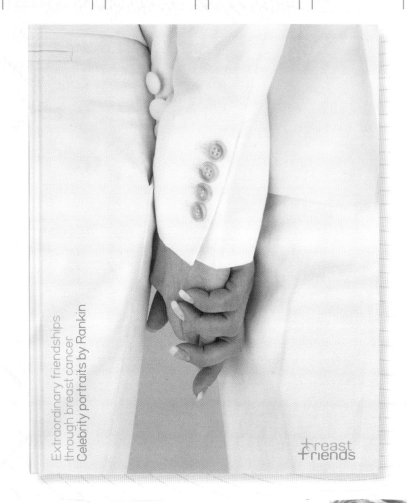

Design: **Kerr | Noble**
Art Direction: **Kerr | Noble**
Photography: **Toby Glanville**
Illustration: **James Graham**
Publisher: **Phaidon**
Country: **UK**

## Breakfast Lunch Tea

Rose Bakery is a Parisian bakery/café, run by Rose Carrarini and her husband Jean-Charles. This book collates 100 of Rose's favorite recipes and encapsulates the essence of the bakery. Responding to her no-fuss approach, Kerr | Noble felt it was important not to overcomplicate the design. "We knew it should be simple and beautiful, in keeping with the values of Rose Bakery," explains Creative Director Amelia Noble, "and we felt it should be a user–friendly, practical book that would inspire people to cook."

For inspiration the designers immersed themselves in French culture (from etiquette to eating to old recipe books) and Parisian café signage and graphics. To differentiate this cookbook from the hundreds of others, they chose a strong typographic approach. The rounded lettering found on Parisian café windows inspired their treatment of the typeface used on the cover. The formal grids and clean lettering of 1930s Parisian posters informed the layout of the back cover and contents page.

The cover features a durable, smooth matte paper, and the inside pages are a slightly off-white matte stock. It has been bound so that it lies flat when opened—again thinking of the practical aspect of reference while cooking.

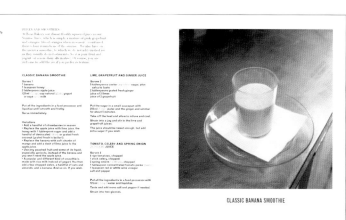

CLASSIC BANANA SMOOTHIE

Design: **Joost Grootens**
Art Direction: **Joost Grootens**
Publisher: **010**
Country: **The Netherlands**

## Metropolitan World Atlas

The Metropolitan World Atlas documents 101 cities and analyzes them through a combination of same-scale ground plans and statistics, with categories ranging from population density to traffic data to air pollution. It was inspired by Arjen van Susteren's graduation project, "Atlas of the Global Pattern," at TU Delft (the Delft University of Technology).

The atlas shows the world's largest metropolitan areas in scale, with comparative data. For readers to understand the complicated information, Grootens created a system of Day-Glo orange dots to represent how each city compares with the others in the book, in any given category.

"It was important to make the map and statistics equal, presenting them on opposite pages. For me, both pages are a map of the city—map and statistics," explains Grootens. "I believe that today, the role of the designer is to structure information in such a way that it is legible and clear. However, its complexity should not be lost through oversimplification. Translating information graphically, especially statistics, can make it more intuitive, more understandable, and, in particular, more interesting."

Four different covers, simplified versions of the maps in the book, were created, each showing a different city: London, Moscow, New York, and Tokyo.

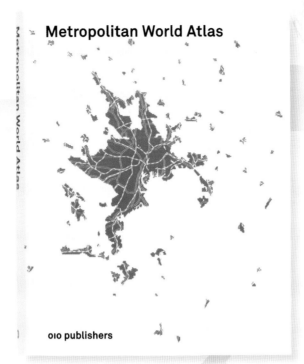

Metropolitan World Atlas

**oıo publishers**

**Metropolitan World Atlas:** Anchorage, Antwerp-Brussels, Athens, Atlanta, Auckland, Baghdad, Bangalore, Bangkok, Barcelona, Beijing, Berlin, Bogotá, Boston, Buenos Aires, Busan, Cairo, Calcutta, Charlotte, Chennai, Chicago, Cincinnati, Copenhagen, Dallas-Ft. Worth, Denver, Detroit, Dhaka, Djakarta, Dubai, Durban, Frankfurt, Geneva, Hamburg, Hong Kong, Houston, Hyderabad, Indianapolis, Istanbul, Jerusalem-Tel Aviv, Johannesburg, Kaohsiung, Karachi, Kinshasa, Kobe-Osaka-Kyoto, Kuala Lumpur, Lagos, Lahore, Las Vegas, Le Havre, Lima, Lisbon, London, Los Angeles, Louisville, Madrid, Manila, Melbourne, Memphis, Mexico City, Miami, Milan, Minneapolis-St.Paul, Monterey, Montreal, Moscow, Mumbai, Nagoya, New Delhi, New Orleans, New York, Orlando, Oslo, Paris, Perth, Philadelphia, Phoenix, Pittsburgh, Randstad Holland, Rhine-Ruhr, Rio de Janeiro, Rome, Sacramento, San Francisco-Oakland, Santiago de Chile, São Paulo, Seattle, Seoul-Incheon, Shanghai, Singapore, St. Louis, St. Petersburg, Stockholm, Sydney, Taichung, Taipei, Tangier, Tehran, Tianjin, Tokyo-Yokohama, Toronto, Vancouver and Washington-Baltimore.

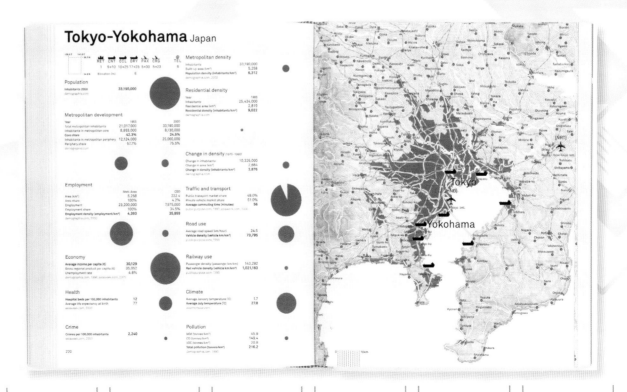

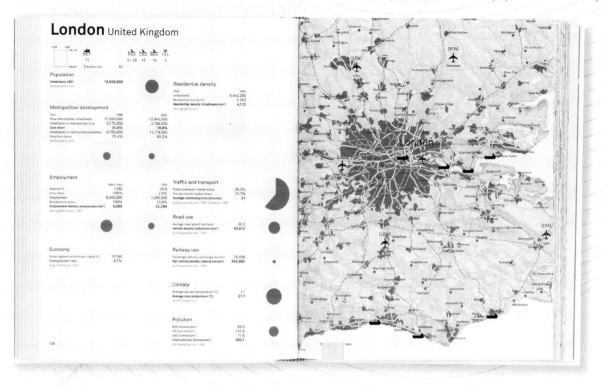

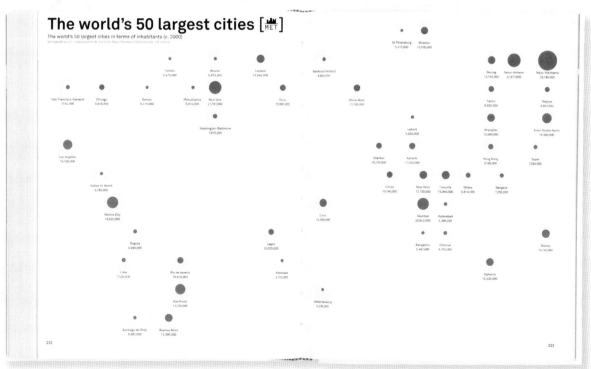

Design: **No Days Off**
Photography: **Wolfgang Tillmans**
Editor: **Polly Clayden**
Publisher: **Taschen**
Country: **UK**

## Why We Must Provide HIV Treatment Information

This book is the result of a global treatment-literacy meeting about HIV, held in Cape Town, South Africa. The aim of the meeting was to review existing treatment-literacy materials and plan ways in which to improve them. It takes the form of quotes from, and portraits of, people affected by or treating HIV in developing countries.

The main idea of the design was to keep it simple and clear, to make the words legible and not intrude on the pictures. The subject matter is delicate, so the design is intended to be sympathetic. "We came up with a simple four-column grid and made all the body copy hang from a line approximately one-quarter from the top of the page," explains Duffy. "This meant that we could employ a stacking system for the details of the interviewees in the top quarter of each page, and also use the line for images to hang off on the double-page spreads containing information."

The stacking of titles and birthplaces was used so that people on previous spreads could be identified without running any copy over the images. Akzidenz Grotesk was used throughout in medium weight, together with three simple, bold colors: black, dark red, and pure magenta.

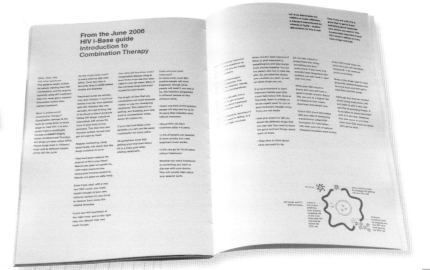

Design: **Nick Bell and David Valdeby**
**at Nick Bell Design**
Art Direction: **Nick Bell**
Publisher: **Tate Publishing**
Country: **UK**

## Tate Modern Art series

This series focuses on the key works of selected artists. The books include essays on each artist's approach. The brief was to create a visually arresting design format that could be used across the text-heavy series.

"This is a design format for a series, therefore inspiration from the content of each book is limited," explains Bell. "Our desire was to create a format for a series that would still look fresh five years later."

The resultant book manages to structure the essays around the key-work pages, which use oversized text and tinted pages for contrast against the essays. The aim was to ensure the key-work pages were as clean and uncluttered as possible—images were sized to fit the full page width wherever possible.

All cover images are details of a piece of the artist's work that the designers thought contained archetypal elements that distinguish their oeuvre. Ringli typeface was used for display text, DTL Documenta for main text, and Scala Sans for captions. A thick varnish was used on the white initials—a distinctive feature of the covers—to give the appearance of screen printing.

Design: **Base Design**
Editor: **Okwui Enwezor**
Publishers: **BIACS/BOM**
Country: **Spain**

## The Unhomely

This book was created for the second International Biennial of Contemporary Art in Seville. The biennial was devoted to the exploration of social disturbances around the world. Printed in English and Spanish editions, the idea behind the design is to "reveal the hidden meaning behind what we see at first glance."

"We wanted to translate the hidden meanings, disturbances, and unsettling nature of a lot of the work presented in the exhibition into the visual identity of this book through typography and the idea of concealing and revealing layers," explain the team at Base Design.

This was the inspiration for folding over the top right corner of the cover, and selected pages throughout the book, to reveal text or imagery on the next page. The imagery featured is that of the participating artists, including Ahlam Shibli, Josephine Meckseper, James Casebere, Maria Eichhorn, Toba Khedoori, and Andreas Slominski.

The designers used different grid systems in which to set the variety of work featured in the book. A wide margin was used for all paintings and text, a tight margin for pages with photography, and a full-bleed format for pages featuring sculpture and installation. Gotham typeface was used for the covers, chapter titles, essay titles, and captions, with DTL Documenta for the essays.

Design: **Paulus M. Dreibholz**
Art Direction: **Paulus M. Dreibholz**
Publisher: **Gaffa Ltd.**
Country: **UK**

## Popper

This book is all about the typeface Popper, designed by Dreibholz. The foundation for its unconventional design is the underlying angular grid, which allows only a limited number of stroke angles and directions.

Originally part of the project Mapping Typography, in which Dreibholz undertook some mapping experiments with type, it soon developed into a separate project, which this book celebrates.

"I wanted the perfect environment to display the typeface and create a truly typographic experience," explains Dreibholz. "My intention was for the book to be humble and modest. Like the early pocket books by Aldus Manutius, published during the Renaissance in Venice, it follows old and established typographic arrangements."

This type-specimen book attempts to honor the typeface as much as the letters themselves. Hardbound with a warm gray cloth cover and red endpapers, it was printed as a limited edition of three.

PIERRE ALBERT-BIROT  *Mon ami Kronos*

PIERRE
ALBERT-BIROT
*Mon ami*
*Kronos*

Z

Design: **David Pearson**
Art Direction: **David Pearson**
Publisher: **Editions Zulma**
Countries: **UK/France**

## Contemporary Fiction series

This is Editions Zulma's progressive Contemporary Fiction series. Pearson was commissioned to design the series after Zulma's Director Laure Leroy saw his work on Penguin's Great Ideas.

Pearson used abstract imagery and repeating patterns for the covers, with the choice for each particular title inspired by its content. "I very much enjoy employing abstraction and symbolism in my work," explains Pearson. "I believe it to be much more engaging for the reader when a design merely hints at the book's contents and allows them to fill in the blanks. I prefer not to dress covers in literal imagery," he adds. "Typographic or pattern-led covers challenge the reader to project meaning onto them."

The covers were printed on a tactile stock that absorbs and softens the colors printed on it. The triangle holding the title on each cover has been subtly debossed. The books themselves are stitched, glued, and have folding flaps.

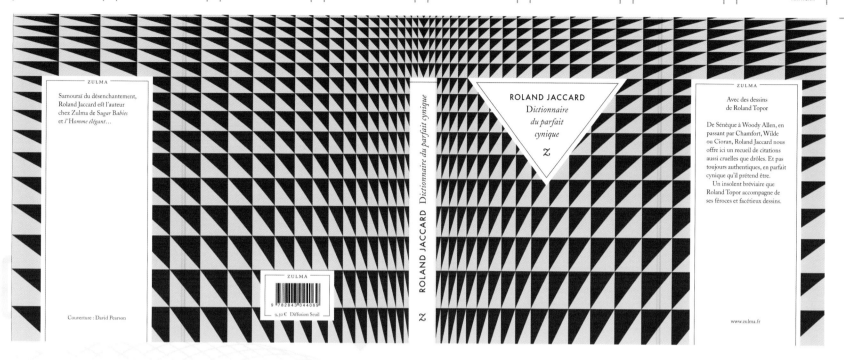

ZULMA

Samouraï du désenchantement, Roland Jaccard est l'auteur chez Zulma de *Sugar Babies* et *l'Homme élégant*…

Couverture : David Pearson

ROLAND JACCARD *Dictionnaire du parfait cynique*

ROLAND JACCARD
*Dictionnaire
du parfait
cynique*

Z

ZULMA

9,50 € Diffusion Seuil

ZULMA

Avec des dessins de Roland Topor

De Sénèque à Woody Allen, en passant par Chamfort, Wilde ou Cioran, Roland Jaccard nous offre ici un recueil de citations aussi cruelles que drôles. Et pas toujours authentiques, en parfait cynique qu'il prétend être.

Un insolent bréviaire que Roland Topor accompagne de ses féroces et facétieux dessins.

www.zulma.fr

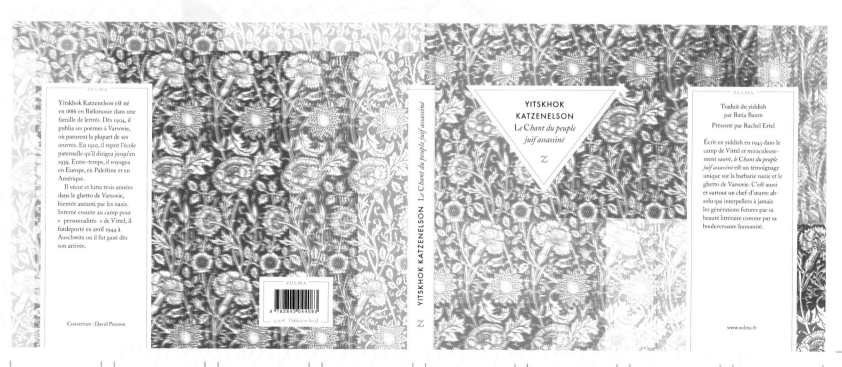

ZULMA

Yitskhok Katzenelson est né en 1886 en Biélorussie dans une famille de lettrés. Dès 1904, il publia ses poèmes à Varsovie, où parurent la plupart de ses œuvres. En 1910, il reprit l'école paternelle qu'il dirigea jusqu'en 1939. Entre-temps, il voyagea en Europe, en Palestine et en Amérique.

Il vécut et lutta trois années dans le ghetto de Varsovie, bientôt anéanti par les nazis. Interné ensuite au camp pour « personnalités » de Vittel, il futdéporté en avril 1944 à Auschwitz où il fut gazé dès son arrivée.

Couverture : David Pearson

YITSKHOK KATZENELSON *Le Chant du peuple juif assassiné*

YITSKHOK
KATZENELSON
*Le Chant du peuple
juif assassiné*

Z

ZULMA

9,50 € Diffusion Seuil

ZULMA

Traduit du yiddish par Batia Baum
Présenté par Rachel Ertel

Écrit en yiddish en 1943 dans le camp de Vittel et miraculeusement sauvé, *le Chant du peuple juif assassiné* est un témoignage unique sur la barbarie nazie et le ghetto de Varsovie. C'est aussi et surtout un chef-d'œuvre absolu qui interpellera à jamais les générations futures par sa beauté littéraire comme par sa bouleversante humanité.

www.zulma.fr

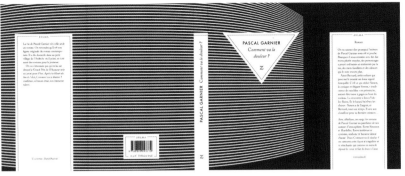

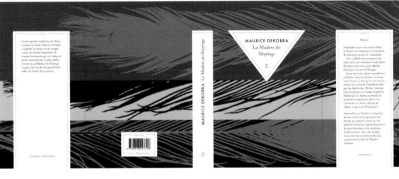

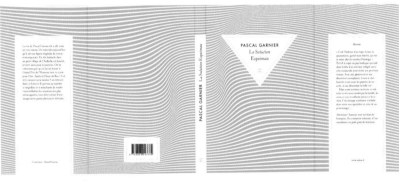

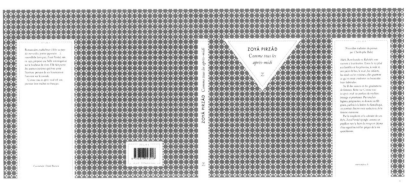

Design: **Paulus M. Dreibholz**
Art Direction: **Paulus M. Dreibholz**
Editors: **Martina Kandeler-Fritsch/**
 **Thomas Kramer**
Publisher: **Hatje Cantz**
Countries: **UK/Austria/Germany**

## Get Off of my Cloud

<u>Get Off of my Cloud</u> is an extensive collection of essays, interviews, comments, transcriptions, and other texts by and about Wolf D. Prix, the lead architect of COOP HIMMELB(L)AU.

"Knowing Wolf D. Prix, it was clear that the content of the book needed to be reflected in the form and format of the book," explains Dreibholz. "It had to be brutal and honest.

"It was a lucky coincidence that the company's corporate identity typeface was Akzidenz Grotesk, which, through its variety in weights and sober appearance, lends itself perfectly to the powerful and pragmatic aspects of the text," he adds. Charter was also used throughout the book, which was printed in both German and English.

The first and last pages are sky blue—the corporate color of COOP HIMMELB(L)AU ("himmelblau" means sky blue in English).

The typographic cover is a deconstructed arrangement of the title. Dynamic and asymmetric, it remains stable on the page. The design references Futurism and Constructivism, movements that have been influential on Prix's work. The cover was laminated to make it durable.

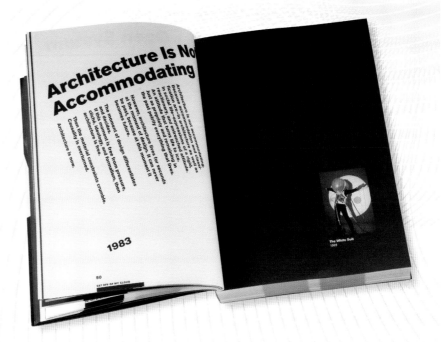

Design: **RDYA Design Group**
Art Direction: **Ricardo Drab**
Publisher: **Ricardo Drab y Asociados**
Country: **Argentina**

## Diseño + Ideas

This book is all about experimental design. Put together by the Buenos Aires–based RDYA Design Group, it includes the work of 30 RDYA designers and their collaborations with different national and international colleagues.

"During the design process designers generate a lot of ideas; some of them will be part of the final project, some will not. This book contains the work that was created during the design process."

The book was printed offset and contains eight different types of paper stock: colored, gloss, matte, and vegetable paper. The graffiti-style typeface on the cover was created using a combination of vector drawing and graffiti sketches.

Design: **Nick Bell Design**
Art Direction: **Nick Bell**
Publisher: **Universities UK**
Country: **UK**

## EurekaUK

Launched by Universities UK at the Science Museum in London, <u>EurekaUK</u> is about 100 discoveries and developments made in UK universities from the 1950s to the early 2000s. It aims to show how our world has been transformed as a result. The design brief was to ensure that the book was highly visual.

"The original idea was to include newspaper cuttings recording the full shock impact of the frontiers crossed with each discovery and development," explains Bell. "This proved too time-consuming, but what remained was a newspaper style of immediacy in the typography. We also wrote headlines, standfirsts, and pull quotes to make the texts more accessible and visual."

For the cover, the designers used a section of text from the Introduction. Knockout typeface was used for the headlines because of its newsy feel, and Bodoni Egyptian was used for the body text. An uncoated paper stock was chosen to provide bulk.

EurekaUK

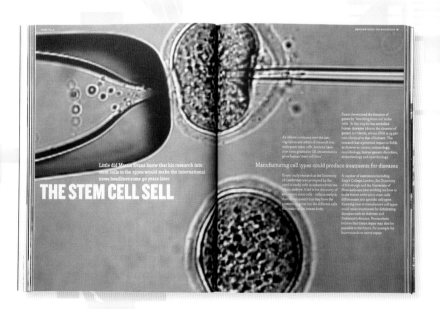

TAKE A PILL, UNDERGO AN OPERATION, HAVE A BABY, GO TO SCHOOL, RECEIVE A BENEFIT, SURF THE INTERNET, TAKE A JOURNEY BY PLANE, TRAIN OR AUTOMOBILE, PLAY A CD, PHONE OVERSEAS, HEAR A WEATHER FORECAST, FOLLOW A ROAD SIGN, GIVE UP SMOKING, STUDY THE STARS...

THE STEM CELL SELL

# IMMACULATE CONCEPTION

On the night of 25 July 1978 medical history was created. A 5lb 12oz baby called Louise Joy Brown was born at 11:47pm by Caesarean section at Oldham General Hospital.

The 1960s: We said, 'In the future, infertile couples will have babies'

Louise was the first 'test-tube baby' created by in vitro fertilisation (IVF) where a mother's egg and father's sperm are fused outside the body in a laboratory.

University of Cambridge embryologist, Robert Edwards and the Oldham-based gynaecologist, Patrick Steptoe, were the first to develop the IVF technique, to enable infertile women to have babies.

They were able to find a reliable way of fertilising a woman's egg in a laboratory test tube and then implanting the newly created embryo in a womb, where it developed into a baby nine months later.

A quarter of a century later, it is estimated that worldwide one million people owe their lives to IVF. Doctors now routinely use the technique to help women who have blocked fallopian tubes or other complications preventing normal births. IVF babies, including Louise's sister Natalie, have gone on to conceive their own healthy babies naturally.

## LASTING EFFECTS

We have under-estimated the long-term psychological impact of floods

The instant catastrophic impact of flooding was brutally exposed by the tsunami disaster in late 2004, one of the world's worst natural disasters. But researchers at Middlesex University have shown that this is really just the start of the problems: people suffer from stress, sleeping problems and depression long after the flood-waters have receded.

## LOOKING BACK IN TIME

## Darren Wall, Faber Design, UK

**What and when was the first book you designed?**
An illustration I did at college was spotted at my university show and used on the cover for <u>Flight</u> by Victoria Glendinning. The publishers, Simon & Schuster, then offered me work experience, which is how I got into book design.

**When approaching book design, what inspires you?**
I grew up on a healthy, geeky diet of Peter Saville and Designers Republic record sleeves so my original inspiration came from music design. Now I try to take influence from as many sources as possible, particularly things that are not related to the book-design industry—fine art, fashion, etc.

**What is your favorite book cover/overall package design?**
John Gray's design for <u>Extremely Loud and Incredibly Close</u> by Jonathan Safran Foer because it annoys me every time I look at it; it's so effortlessly simple and beautiful.

**What makes a good book cover?**
That ridiculous feeling that you have to buy the book immediately, irrespective of the contents, because it looks so damn lovely.

**How much of a role do you think the designer plays as a marketer in the retail environment?**
We have to pay close attention to the needs of our marketing department, as the cover is hugely important in selling the book both to retailers and the customer. At Faber we have the honor of being encouraged to produce groundbreaking covers to distinguish our books from those of other publishers.

**What are the best and worst things about designing books?**
The best thing: when someone tells you they bought a book just for the cover. The worst thing: changing spine widths, which sounds just as achingly boring as it is.

**How would you design a book if there were no limit to budget?**
I think, actually, the most exciting design briefs are the most restricted ones. I'd much rather be told I have to design a cheap paperback in two colors that can't have any imagery on it than be told I have no limits. That said, I've always wanted to use lenticular, so I'd plump for that if I had a huge budget.

**Do you judge a book by its cover?**
Yes, to the point of near-tearful hysteria when browsing bookstores for something to actually read.

## Jonathan Ellery, Browns, UK

**What and when was the first book you designed?**
It was in 1999 and was called <u>Flowers</u>. It was for the photographer Martin Parr and a Swedish paper client to promote a brand of paper.

**When approaching book design, what inspires you?**
If it's for someone else, then it's the work of the artist or photographer I'm doing it with. I have to relate to and like the work of the individual to take the project on in the first place. If it's one of my own books, for me, then it's the sheer joy and freedom of being able to design and publish it, to liberate an idea and get it on a bookshelf. Thereafter it's a continuing love affair with paper, inks, the production process, pace, rhythm, and edit.

**What is your favorite book cover/overall package design?**
I don't have an individual favorite. I like looking at lots of books on shelves. I find it very revealing about a person.

**What makes a good book cover?**
I really don't know. I was going to say simplicity, which is generally how I approach my books, but then again a lot of the books on my shelves are quite complex aesthetically. I find the book covers that Fuel (now Damon Murray and Stephen Sorrell) has been designing over the years for the photographer Juergen Teller intriguing and very beautiful. They're quite uncomfortable. Another of my favorites would be <u>Punk Picasso</u> by Larry Clark.

**How much of a role do you think the designer plays as a marketer in the retail environment?**
For me it's all part of it. Every book I've ever designed I've launched in some way, either with an accompanying exhibition or a launch event. We've launched books in galleries, restaurants, a derelict brewery, a Freemasons' temple, a deserted warehouse on the outskirts of Paris, a church in New York—in fact, anywhere that has an unlikely relationship with the book itself. It's rewarding and a good way of getting interesting people together and having fun.

**What are the best and worst things about designing books?**
I like the smell of beautifully printed books, but hate how long it takes to print and bind. Patience is not one of my virtues.

**How would you design a book if there were no limit to budget?**
I would show restraint; a no-limit budget does not equate to a good book. In fact, it can be quite the opposite.

**Do you judge a book by its cover?**
Yes.

## 04

"What inspires me is a continuing love affair
with paper, inks, the production process ..."

Jonathan Ellery, UK

# Printing & Finishing

"I'd much rather be told I have to design a cheap paperback in two colors that can't have any imagery on it than be told I have no limits."

Darren Wall, UK

# Introduction

As with all the work included in this book, this chapter shows how designers have an almost unlimited range of options in creating books and book packages that are different from the norm. One way to make a book stand out is by using unusual materials and/or innovative printing techniques. From embossed covers to die cuts to foil blocking, such touches can make a book that extra bit special. The following pages contain some great examples of how this can be done.

Design: **Rinzen**
Art Direction: **Rilla Alexander**
Publisher: **Victionary**
Countries: **Australia/Germany**

## Neighbourhood

Neighbourhood was initiated by design collective Rinzen, bringing together artists from around the world in a "spontaneous collaborative toy remixing project." Beginning with the blank canvas of a featureless cloth toy, each designer was asked to create a character, whether through stitching, painting, drawing, accessorizing, tailoring, or even adding or removing body parts.

"The toy was then returned to us to be photographed before being passed on to the next participant, weaving a global trail of inspiration, thread, blood, stuffing, and love," explains Alexander. "This process was repeated over and over, yielding an entire neighborhood, the inhabitants of which are finally revealed in this lovingly crafted family album."

The felt cover has embroidered patches that represent the countries the toys visited on their global travels. Full-page photographs of each toy sit opposite details of its painting and stitching, etc.

"Due to the handmade nature of the remixing, we felt it was important that the design of the book be solid and simple, but imbued with the friendliness and personality that make the project what it is," adds Alexander.

The tangled-threads motif on the cover is continued within the book and forms the custom-designed typography that introduces each sequence: the double-page spread openers have a centered quote from one of the participants with a photo of the toy in its original form on the facing page.

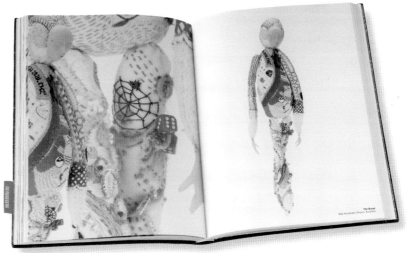

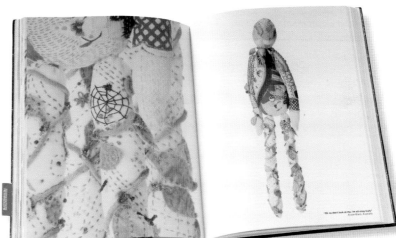

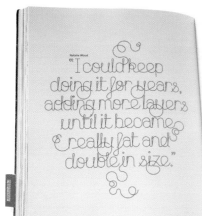

Design: **SEA**
Art Direction: **SEA**
Photography: **Rankin**
Publisher: **Dazed Books**
Country: **UK**

## TuuliTastic

TuuliTastic showcases a collection of
commissioned fashion photographs
along with advertising and editorial
images, all of Rankin's muse, Tuuli.
All were taken over a three-year period.
The book, structured according to style of
shot rather than chronologically, moves
from seductive black-and-white editorial
through to sumptuous color portraits.

"To give the editorial structure pace, we
introduced spreads that break from the
grid and offer a more layered, scattered
layout that works well with the more
intimate, personal shots," explains Judge.

The black-and-gold silkscreen silhouette
that wraps around the cover was inspired
by an early James Bond poster, for
Goldfinger. The cover is bound in gold
cloth with gold foil blocking used to apply
the text. Futura Extra Bold and Light were
used throughout.

Design: **Underware/BuroLamp**
Publisher: **Self-published**
Country: **The Netherlands**

## De Illusie 1991–2006

In the city of the Hague, in the Netherlands, is De Illusie, a house that has been used by squatters for more than 15 years. The building hosts concerts, exhibitions, lectures, and performances, and is also home and workplace to 25 people, including the members of Underware. De Illusie is a celebration of this house, covering the events that it has hosted. The cover itself lists these, from 1991 through to 2006. To accommodate the entire list, a foldout cover was created.

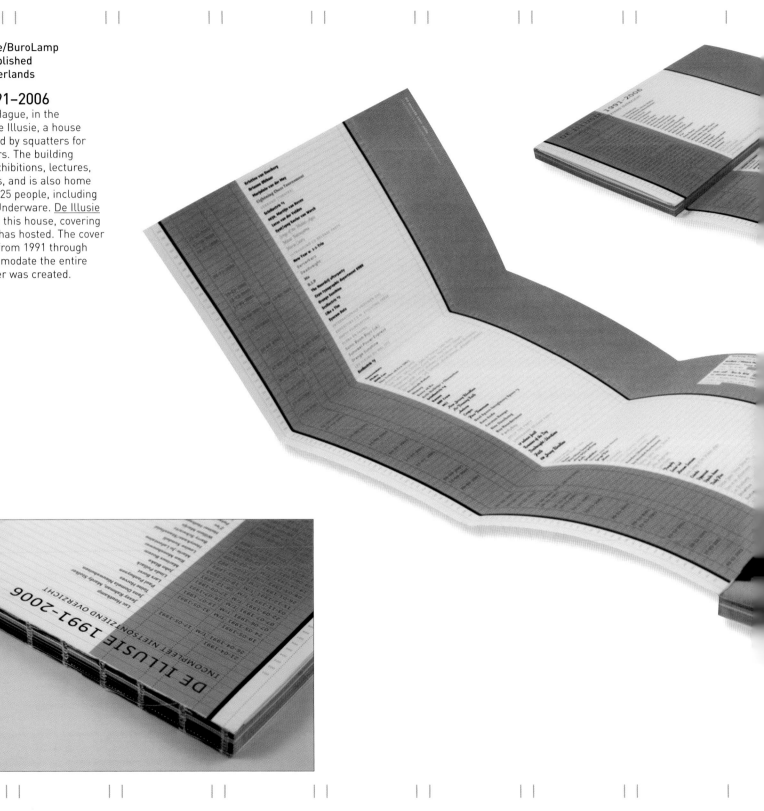

NIEK DE MEER (1970) WOONT IN LA ILLUSIE

Is zelfstandig metaalbewerker en heeft o.a. meege-
werkt aan het ontwikkelen van de tegelkachel, maakte
een paardenoperatietafel en realiseerde kunstobject
Palm. Zijn metaalbewerkingsbedrijf Laskracht is
gevestigd in de Grote Pyr.

www.laskracht.nl

RONJA STROOVOGEL (2002) DOCHTER VAN ESTHER EN NIEK

Ronja Stroovogel is geboren in het Bronovo zieken-
huis en woont sindsdien in De Illusie. Zingen doet ze
graag en sinds kort gaat ze naar de peuterspeelzaal.

Design: **Geoff Kaplan/Gail Swanlund**
Art Direction: **General Working Group/**
**Stripe LA**
Publisher: **Prestel Verlag/San Jose**
**Museum of Art**
Country: **USA**

# Jennifer Steinkamp

This book was created on the occasion of a mid-career retrospective of artist Jennifer Steinkamp. Geoff Kaplan of General Working Group and Gail Swanlund of Stripe LA collaborated with Steinkamp to realize this project. The book's design is informed by the kinetic qualities of Steinkamp's work, with design elements reflecting the back narratives of each piece.

The cover features a lenticular image of Steinkamp's "Rapunzel," with 3-D bubblegum-style typography created especially for the cover by Steinkamp.

"Throughout, the book's orientation switches from portrait to landscape as a play on the idea of moving between reading spreads and looking through windows into the work," explain Kaplan and Swanlund. "Additionally, we asked Jennifer for references and inspirations for each piece of work. Jennifer's titles are usually taken from songs, movies, and literature. We pooled all the nouns from her references and converted them into drawings. At the back of the book, just before the German translation, on pink stock, we put an annotated index that keys the drawings to her works."

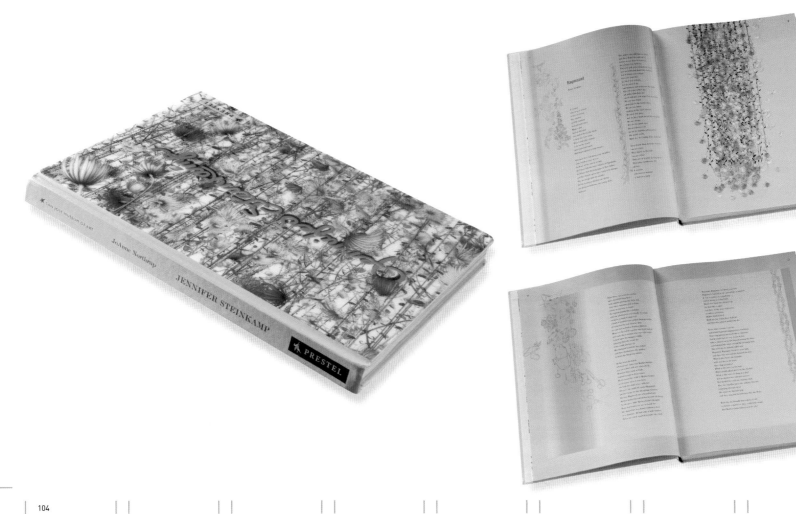

Design: **Rafael Koch**
Art Direction: **Rafael Koch**
Illustration: **Peter Radelfinger**
Publisher: **Verlag für moderne
Kunst Nürnberg**
Countries: **Switzerland/Germany**

## Hin und Her

Hin und Her is based on a visual
and textual interpretation of human
relationships. With no brief as such, the
design is the result of close teamwork
between illustrator, author, and designer.

"The design follows the aesthetics of the
content," explains Koch. "The drawings
were arranged to make longer and
shorter image sequences telling stories
about human relationships. Textually, the
author's choice to use letters, postcards,
texts, and e-mails as media to transport
the written contents also influenced the
design—the texts were set in only one
row, from top to bottom. We chose
Lineto's Superstudio, by Jon Hares,
for the font as it matched the aesthetics
of the images." French folds were used
throughout the book to ensure that the
drawings have no show through.

For the cover, a white, embossed carton
structured like skin was used. For the
inside pages, two different paper stocks
were chosen—slightly shiny poster paper
for the drawings, and bright white office
paper for the text—to differentiate further
between the visual and written content.

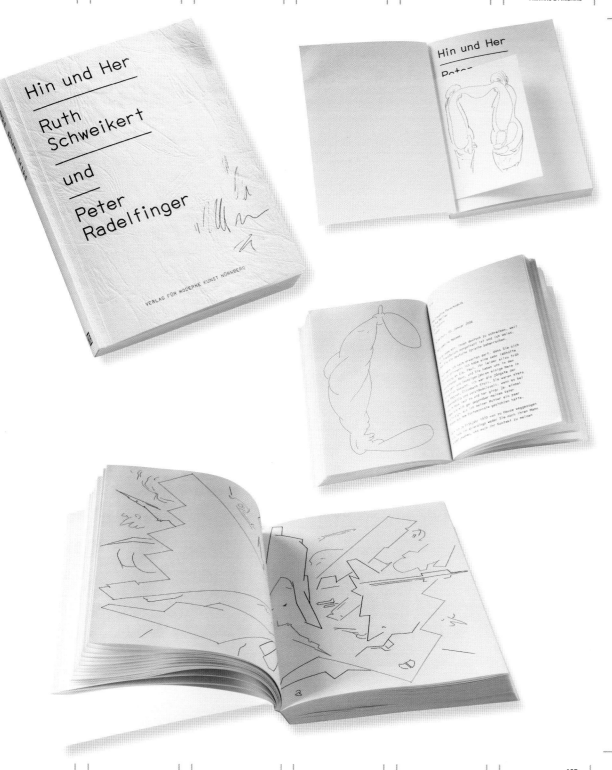

Design: **Gabor Palotai**
Art Direction: **Gabor Palotai**
Illustration: **Gabor Palotai**
Publisher: **Gabor Palotai Publishers**
Country: **Sweden**

## Odysseus

Palotai's Odysseus is not the usual novel with words, but instead a "graphic novel" in which text has been replaced by the visual. "The aim was to create a 'bible,'" explains Palotai, "a graphic design novel where the storyteller is the reader and their own Odysseus."

In Greek mythology Odysseus spent his life on a journey, every trace of which became an endless narrative to be retold and reinterpreted. Based on this, Odysseus: A Graphic Design Novel is a verbal voyage whereby the storyteller makes up the storytelling and is, at the same time, the listener interpreting his or her own story. Only the chapter titles suggest what has taken place, but they never say what is happening.

The images in the book are a retrospective collection of Palotai's illustrations. The inside pages are 170gsm Arctic Gloss and the cover is nylon velvet with gold typography. Published as part of a personal art project, it is a bold and unusual title with great design execution.

Design: **Hörður Lárusson**
Publisher: **Self-published**
Country: **Iceland**

## Þe Búkk

Þe Búkk was born from Hörður Lárusson's desire to make a book from scratch, following it through from idea to production. "I decided to contact some friends, most of them graphic designers, and ask them to create material for one or more pages of the book," he explains. "They could do whatever they wanted," he adds. "The only restriction was that they put their name somewhere on the page, in Helvetica, my favorite typeface." This is the only typeface used throughout the book. Lárusson kept the overall design simple so as not to overshadow the work. The book, printed in a limited run of 100 copies, is hand-bound.

Design: **SEA**
Art Direction: **SEA**
Photography: **Rankin**
Publisher: **GF Smith**
Country: **UK**

## Surface Seduction

<u>Surface Seduction</u> promotes GF Smith's PhoenixMotion paper stock. The imagery used—close-ups of skin—reflects the surface qualities of the paper. "We called it <u>Surface Seduction</u> as this referred both to the images and to the paper," explains Jones. "The shots included are very ambiguous. They're meant to keep you guessing as to what you're looking at. We wanted the images to work alongside the paper's surface, because the paper is as important as Rankin's photography.

"The aim of the book was to sell more paper, using stunning images, printed beautifully, on amazing paper, so we wanted a large format to get as much surface printed as possible," adds Jones. "We calculated the largest book format that could be physically printed on a B1 press (707 x 1,000mm [27¹³/₁₆ x 39³/₈in])."

Several different printing and finishing techniques were used to create the book, including a red gloss foil, matte laminates, halftone neutral seals, spot gloss varnishes, and overall gloss varnishes. A condensed version of Helvetica has been used throughout, in an eight-column grid.

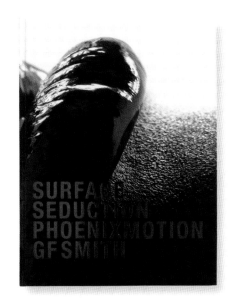

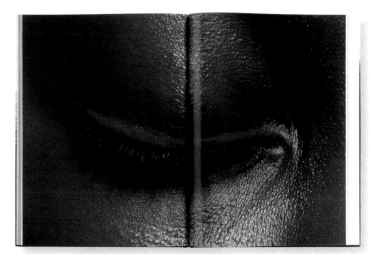

Art Direction: **Clare Skeats**
Design: **Clare Skeats**
Publisher: **Portobello Books**
Country: **UK**

## A Fairy Find

This is a humorous, eccentric book about a parallel universe inhabited by fairies, written and illustrated by painter, publisher, and moviemaker Andrew Lanyon. Skeats explains, "This commission was unusual in that I was presented with three of Lanyon's photocopied, hand-stitched, self-published volumes. Portobello wanted me to combine them in one distinctive book package." Lanyon also gave Skeats images to use in this book. They consisted of an eclectic collection of found ephemera, ranging from scientific diagrams to engravings to 1950s advertising images.

The cover design is Skeats' response to her initial read-through of the three volumes. She used a dark blue cloth with a silver foil stamp. "Lanyon seemed to be suggesting that fairies are these omnipresent, mischievous, capricious beings that exert a huge influence on us as humans," she explains. "This, together with the fact that I wanted the visual style of the cover to reference some of the diagrammatical imagery inside, inspired me to start looking at astronomy maps to come up with the final design."

Lanyon wanted to retain the original centered layout and pagination as far as possible. Skeats did reduce the width of the measure and make the margins symmetrical and generous, with centered running heads and folios, but deliberately avoided imposing any radical changes on the design.

Design: **3 Deep Design**
Art Direction: **3 Deep Design**
Photography: **Paul Knight**
Publisher: **3 Deep Publishing**
Country: **Australia**

## Material by Product

Material by Product is a Melbourne-based fashion label run by Susan Dimasi and Chantal McDonald. It uses two conceptually original fashion design systems: Punch Out and Waste Collation. This highly crafted publication represents the principles of these design systems graphically. It also documents the history of the practice and thinking behind each Material by Product collection.

The designers used a classic grid, original hand-drawn typography, and a tactile and oversized cover. Gold foil blocking was applied to the cover to bring energy and focus to the typography. For the pages 150gsm silk stock was used, with 250gsm uncoated stock for the eight-page gatefold cover.

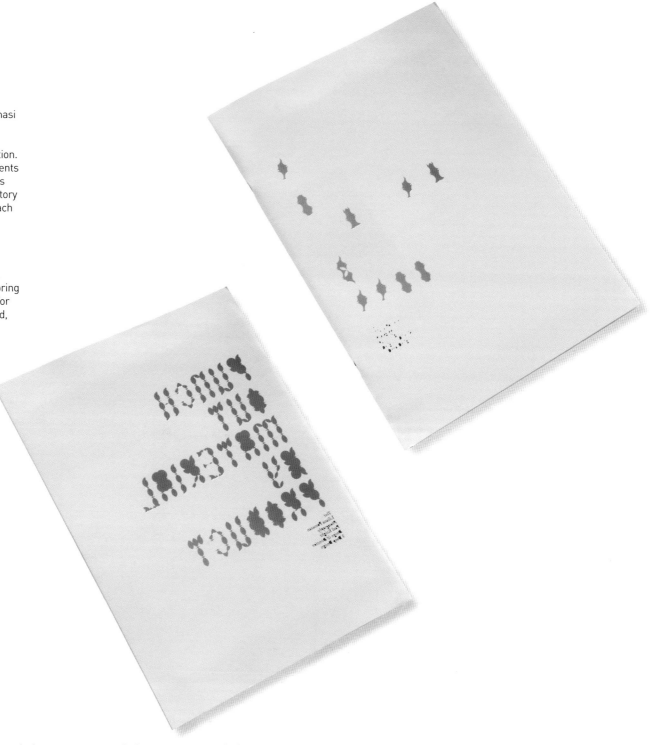

Design: **Base Design**
Editor: **Tony Delcampe**
Publishers: **BOM/La Cambre Mode[s]**
Country: **Belgium**

## La Cambre Mode[s]
## 1986–2006

Base worked in collaboration with La Cambre Mode[s], the Fashion department at Belgium's National School of Visual Arts of La Cambre, on this celebration of the school's 20th anniversary. "The aim was to make a book that wasn't superficial," explain the team at Base Design. "We wanted the book to show the energy, education, and creativity of the school."

The school asked students, both old and new, to submit imagery for inclusion in the book. From these the school and Base selected the final imagery, which ranges from drawings to photographs to sketches. The concept behind the design was the notion of a sketchbook.

Six different paper stocks were used in the production of the book, from uncoated to gloss, and the cover is embossed.

Elisabeth Paillié, *journalist*

It was as a jury member that I discovered La Cambre, following an invitation from Francine Pairon. Yet from the very strong creativity that the department reveals, I think that the main strength of the teaching staff is that it encourages individual development. The end of the year shows aren't reduced to a single tone, rather you see personalities coming through. La Cambre also has a strong presence in international contexts. Because of this I was able to discover Sandrina Fasoli at Hyères. Her work has made impressive progress. Her collection for spring-summer 2007 was perfect and would not be out of place in all the department shows. She has a distinctive view of femininity that incorporates an unusual visual elegance and playfulness. Turning to a completely different approach, I was also very moved by Eva Gronbach's last collection. It was built around the work outfits of the miners of the site in the German city of Essen that was closed down in recent years and has been put on the UNESCO World Heritage List. Eva bought the clothes to rework them. This reinterpretation has resulted in some unique pieces which were all the more poignant because of their history.

Through the years other names have also had an impact on me. Now we are all familiar with Cathy Pill's work: her graphic researches, her use of volume, the fluidity of her garments. Isabelle Lenfant should make a breakthrough as her work is accomplished, ultra-refined with a slight 'rock' touch that makes her stand out. Both graduated in 2006, Armand Michaux and Anthony Vaccarello are good examples of two universes that coexist in the same academic year and are utterly different. Armand Michaux presented a collection that was close to design, where clothes became a sort of fluid architecture, whereas Anthony Vaccarello showcases an incredible talent for craft through his plaited leather works which are almost sculptural and very sensuous.

I think that in first and second year there is also some remarkable work done around the concept of volume. The students present very powerful and intriguing pieces that would not look out of place in an art gallery. Furthermore the approach of the students resembles that of visual artists. Their know-how is complemented by their knowledge of clothes. To conclude, La Cambre does not base itself on trends, rather it pushes young talents to express their true nature.

**Interview,** *Justin Morin*

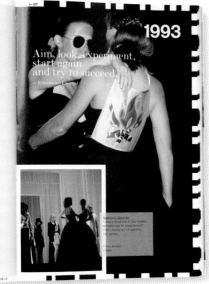

**1993**

Aim, look, experiment,
start again
and try to succeed.
— Emmanuel Laurent

**Nadine Depuydt,** *professor of technique from 1989 until 2004*
Part two

*Is talent always noticeable at first glance?*
Well with people like Sandrine Rombaux or Tony Delcampe, yes. As soon as they set foot in the school, you felt that they had enormous potential, which needed to be channeled of course. But that is the role of the teaching team. A school does not produce talent; talent enters in a school. And when it enters, you see that a student either already has the potential to express the gift he/she has or that they have something in them that they are uncertain how to translate. It's our role to frame it, to open the students' eyes, to enable them to express the talent that they have. When it comes to the entrance exams, you have to be able to choose with precision. It would be a shame not to give a chance to those who deserve it and to bypass talent. But we also have to be able to admit that we make mistakes. One must be capable of making students understand that they are not doing the right thing, that they will suffer for a long time if they try to fit into a place they are not suited for. This is a profession where you cannot place people on the market if they are not talented. Someone with no talent will burn out very quickly in this profession.

*You've worked with two directors of the department with very different styles …*
I spent fifteen years at La Cambre, the first ten with Francine and the five others with Tony. Basically, fifteen happy years! Francine trained my eye, and it sustained me. But because I am a perfectionist, I was always very tense and stressed, afraid not to meet other people's expectations. So when Francine decided to go her separate way, I experienced something extraordinary. The whole team – Tony Delcampe, Eric Beaudouin, Sandrine Rombaux, Solange Thiry – was composed of my former students. And they had become my masters! From the moment that Tony took control, I freed my energy in a more serene environment even though the work carried on unrelentingly. Somehow it was less painful. It gave me back my know-how and the ability to further it. I often think of the saying "Never forget who crowned you queen". I think that is the best way of thanking them.

**Interview,** *Anne-Françoise Moyson*

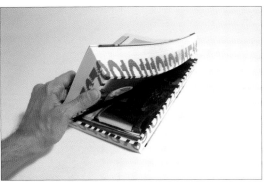

Design: **3 Deep Design**
Art Direction: **3 Deep Design**
Publishers: **3 Deep Publishing/**
    **West Space**
Country: **Australia**

## Formation and Form: West Space 1993–2003

Formation and Form: West Space 1993–2003 chronicles Melbourne-based gallery West Space's active involvement in the presentation of contemporary art and ideas over its first decade. However, it also looks at artist-run activity as a practice in independent action and "do-it-yourself" initiatives that address issues such as government support, survival and growth, and notions of cultural value and social context.

It presents contributors' work in a series of colored folios. The color coding used provides a reference to the sections and the archive. An original typeface from 3 Deep Design was used as a display face, with Helvetica used for all body text, on a classic four-column grid. The cover is 3mm laminated board, and the pages 150gsm Precision uncoated paper stock.

Design: **David Lane/i.o.u./
Eat Sleep Work/Play**
Art Direction: **David Lane**
Publisher: **Self-published**
Country: **UK**

## A Book of One Hundred and Sixty One Students and Their Work

This book is essentially a directory of 161 graduates from the BA Graphic Design department of Central Saint Martins College of Art and Design, London. The brief was to allow each student enough space to portray their character. As the book was to be sent out free to the design and creative industries, the budget was tight.

"Our initial intention was to build physical frameworks for the students to interact with and be portrayed within," explains Lane. "Every spread is a photographic account of the person and the work they produced, thus giving an objective account of this particular year of Graphic Design at Central Saint Martins."

The solution for the cover was simple, but clever—a list of all the participating students and their page numbers. This resolved the issue of how to brand on behalf of 161 aspiring graphic designers. The cover was printed with thermographic ink on matte uncoated paper. Stabilo acted as a sponsor, and each student was invited to highlight their own name and sign 10 books in the space provided on the back. At the graduation show, visitors were given pens and encouraged to highlight names on the cover as they walked through the show.

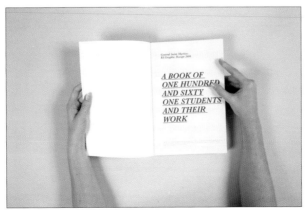

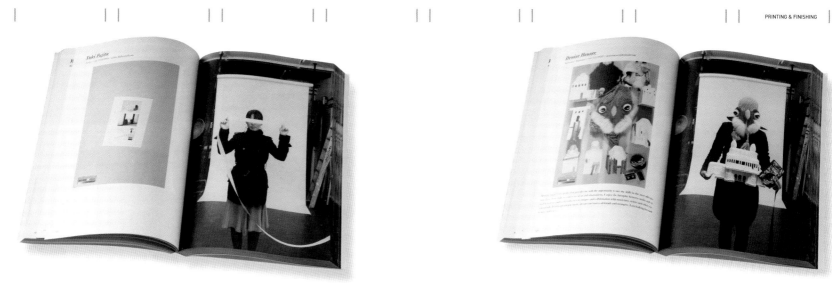

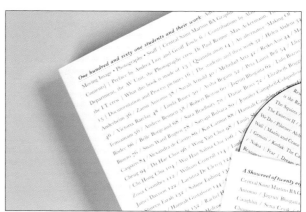

Design: **Chris Rubino and José Parlá**
   **at Studio 1800**
Art Direction: **Chris Rubino**
Publisher: **Spoonfed Publishing**
Country: **USA**

## Cityscapes

Cityscapes is a monograph of Cuban-
American painter José Parlá. The book's
launch coincided with a major exhibition
of Parlá's work during the Art Basel
Miami festival.

The idea was to show the painter's work
in a simple and elegant way. Parlá has
moved from a street-art background into
the fine-art world. The designers wanted
to make sure that his work was presented
in a way that showed the dedication and
time he has put into this transition.

"I looked at some older monographs—
mostly '60s and '70s—and tried to relate
to the style in which they were designed,"
explains Rubino. "I chose a high baseline
to present the artwork. It accentuates
the upward motion of a lot of Parlá's
work. Also, a great majority of the work
is dramatically horizontal in scale; this
baseline allowed the work to sit well in
each layout and provided an open space
to typeset plate titles and sizes."

The cover has a UV coating that aims
to replicate the depth and movement
of Parlá's oil paintings.

Design: **Kjetil Wold at Bleed**
Art Direction: **Kjetil Wold**
Photography: **Chris Harrison**
Publisher: **ALU S.P.A.**
Country: **Norway**

## Leave Your Mark

ALU designs and creates in-store retail systems for clients including Nike, Zara, Fornarina, Nokia, and GAP. This book serves as a promotional tool. Inspired by the nature of ALU's business, the book is built around the idea of "leaving your mark" and how different people do that.

"This concept runs through the book with different levels of metaphors and design solutions," explains Wold. We looked to the street-art scene for inspiration, and also to the way international fashion brands use patterns and repetitions to create a visual experience."

The book is divided into two sections: the first focuses on ALU's brand values and the second on its technical skills. To emphasize this, two different paper stocks have been used—Curious Metallics Cryogen White and Tom & Otto Gloss. Much of the text was handwritten, but Trade Gothic and Century Old Style typefaces were also used. The cover text was applied using a foil emboss.

Design: **Meike Kerstholt**
Art Direction: **Meike Kerstholt**
Publisher: **Meike Kerstholt & De Jager**
Country: **The Netherlands**

# VOLT.A.

This book was designed to support the final presentation of De Jager's graduation project at the Academy of Architecture in Arnhem. <u>VOLT.A.</u> is an architectural plan for the quay at Antwerp Harbor in Belgium.

"In this book I tried to illustrate the visual experience you get while you're strolling, jogging, or driving along the quayside," explains Kerstholt. "The photographs in this book, taken by the quayside, show the many details that can be seen there."

Japanese binding was used to create the book's two "separate" parts: the visual experience and the technical information. On cutting the binding open, De Jager's architectural ideas and plans become clear to the reader.

The cardboard cover is printed with an abstract element of a large photograph taken at the quay. Each of the 35 books printed has a different part of this photo, making them all unique.

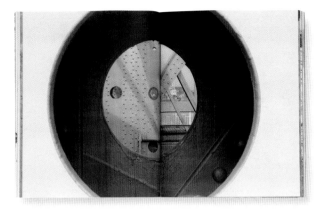

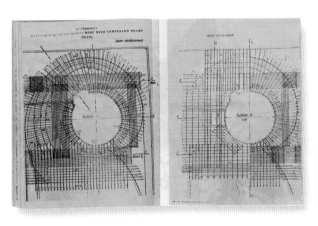

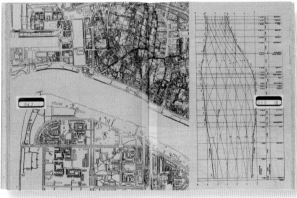

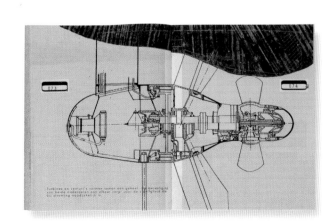

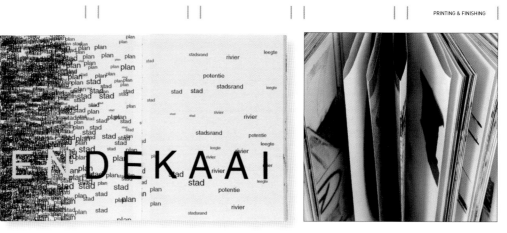

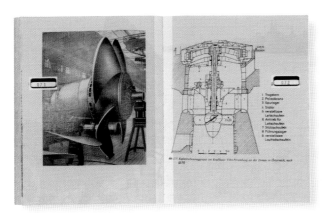

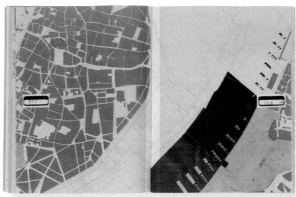

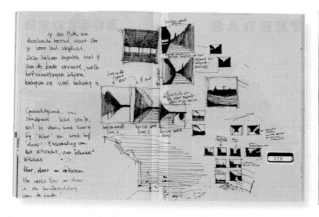

Design: **Surface**
Art Direction: **Surface**
Publisher: **Sternberg Press**
Country: **Germany**

## Bedlam

<u>Bedlam</u> is a novel inspired by a year in the life of Richard Dadd, a Victorian painter and inmate of London's Bethlehem Hospital, more commonly known as Bedlam. As the first title in a series, Surface's design concept does not relate specifically to it, but rather focuses on its functionality within the series of books. As such, several elements, such as the format (130 x 190mm [5⅛ x 7½in]) and the gray linen cover with blue embossed text, have been fixed. However, the color of the prose text will change from title to title.

A one-column grid was used for the prose text, which is set in Lido STF Regular. The book was bound with thread stitching and the page edges set in silver.

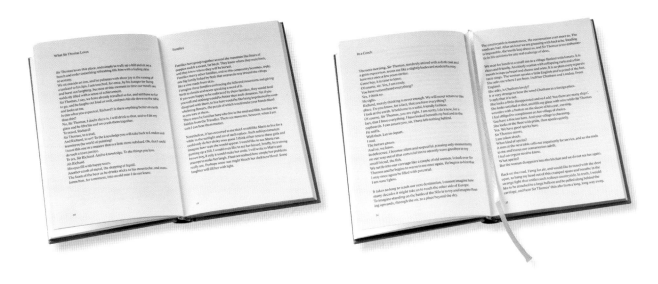

Design: **Lotta Kühlhorn**
Photography: **Pelle Bergström**
Publisher: **Albert Bonnniers Förlag**
Country: **Sweden**

## Vardags Lyx

<u>Vardags Lyx</u>, which means "everyday luxury," celebrates the idea that every day should have some element of luxury to it, and encourages the reader to make their life a little more sumptuous.

"I wanted to create a book that gave readers the same feeling they would get entering a big old luxury perfume store," explains Kühlhorn. "I thought the design elements of such a shop fitted well with the idea of luxury—the roses, gold, pink, the script patterns, and so on."

In keeping with this, Grotesque, Palace Script, and New Baskerville typefaces were used throughout, and the book was covered with Linotex Moire, printed with a luxurious gold-dot pattern.

Design: **Kelly Verhallen**
Art Direction: **Kelly Verhallen**
Photography: **Mike Roelofs**
Publisher: **Kelly Verhallen**
Country: **The Netherlands**

## The Small Home World Atlas

This book was developed by Verhallen to show the impact of globalization on today's world. "The Western human being is becoming a self-assured inhabitant of the world," explains Verhallen. "He or she isn't just an inhabitant of his or her village or city anymore, or a nationality belonging to that city. Therefore, the meaning of 'home' has changed."

The idea was based on Verhallen's own experiences and how she sees the world as a student, designer, woman, and inhabitant of the Netherlands. Imagery forms the book's main content, with illustrations giving the reader a window into the Netherlands. "You don't have to feel like a foreigner in the Netherlands because there are so many nationalities visible in this small country," adds Verhallen. "If you look at the Netherlands through this book you can feel at home in Holland. This is because 'home' is defined by 'contact and recognition,' and the Netherlands is a mix of international influences because of globalization."

The Small Home World Atlas was printed in one piece on a 5m (c. 16½ft) length of paper and then folded into pages. Verhallen chose this method in order to incorporate the content of the book into the design concept. Because of globalization, the world is almost a borderless place—a small world that connects in many ways.

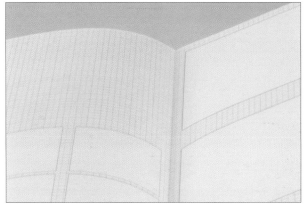

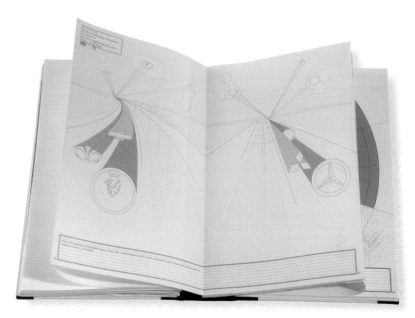

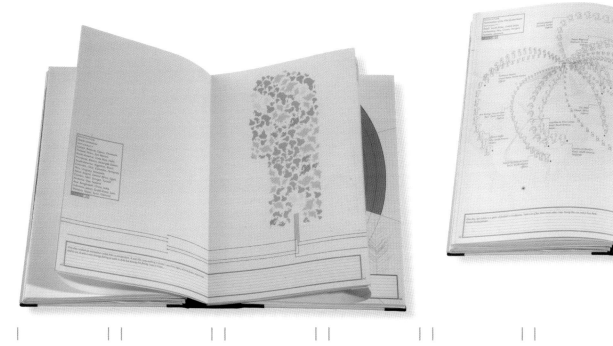

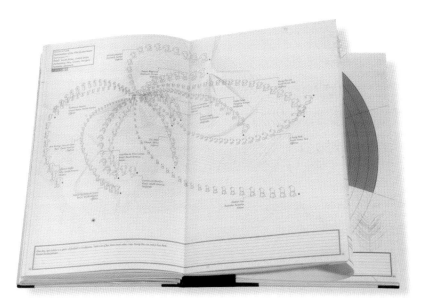

# Joe Marianek, Pentagram, USA

**What and when was the first book you designed?**
My first book was <u>Writing</u> by Marguerite Duras. It was a class assignment at RISD [Rhode Island School of Design]. We were asked to perfect-bind several copies for the final critique. Mine fell apart when the professor picked it up; the glue was still wet. So, the RISD Yearbook was the first real book project I was involved with, in 2003. It was produced in collaboration with four other friends at RISD. There was a bottomless printing budget and we took advantage of it.

**When approaching book design, what inspires you?**
The slow pace, brevity, and mixed messages of slideshows are inspiring. Experiencing these feels like reading a book extremely slowly. I enjoy having to work to construct the meaning, particularly if I don't understand the topic. Also, a lot of graphic novels are fantastic in their sequential story-telling. People like Adrian Tomine, Kikuo Johnson, and Chris Ware know how to entrance readers and move eyes around the page with a few economical lines and some good lettering.

**What is your favorite book cover/overall package design?**
<u>The Circus in the Mist</u> by Bruno Munari. It's the first one I remember reading. The entire book is made up of different paper colors and transparencies, with very abstract textures and shapes used to tell the story of a visit to the circus.

**What makes a good book cover?**
A good book cover is like an honest smile and a firm handshake. Because engaging with a book is a time commitment, you don't want a cover that will swindle you into reading an awful book.

**How much of a role do you think the designer plays as a marketer in the retail environment?**
Good books sell themselves. Their design either enhances their value or plays an ambivalent role. Books are 3-D posters for themselves. Most book designers don't begin with a market-centric intent, as they might with other consumer-product packaging. Generally, books have so few predictable and essential elements, they only stand out from one another by virtue of their design. The established conventions should be broken. I guess if a book is well crafted, intriguing, and perhaps slightly unconventional, people are more likely to pick it up, even if the subject matter wouldn't normally interest them.

**What are the best and worst things about designing books?**
The best thing is being able to add a layer of meaning to the content or contribute to the content on the level of the authors. The worst thing would be designing a book for which you disagreed with the content, or knew that it was dishonest.

**How would you design a book if there were no limit to budget?**
I would create some sort of really big book, at least the size of a human. It would have everything in it. You could hang it on the wall, in a central location with good lighting, and then read it from 3m (10ft) away, from a comfortable chair. The pages would have to be paper and smell like paper. You might need a broomstick to turn the pages. I think such an object could be the center of the house and a substitute for the Internet.

**Do you judge a book by its cover?**
I usually judge a book by its author and publisher; but as far as the cover goes, I just talk about books behind their back.

## David Pearson, David Pearson Design, UK

**What and when was the first book you designed?**
It was for a book design project at college. Rather predictably, I chose to design a cover for <u>Nineteen Eighty-Four</u>. I specifically remember breaking my fax machine while trying to drag sheets of paper through it. The image I used was the only one I managed to prize from its jaws before it died.

**When approaching book design, what inspires you?**
It's almost always the moments when you're not trying that the ideas hit you. I find the (London Underground's) District Line at midnight to be particularly fertile ground.

**What is your favorite book cover/overall package design?**
I recently dug deep and bought a copy of <u>The Sheltering Sky</u> that features an Alvin Lustig cover. It's a masterpiece of composition and symbolism and is unencumbered by any idea of what a book cover is supposed to be. It's pervaded by a real sense of joy and I feel very happy whenever I'm holding it.

**What makes a good book cover?**
Confidence. From the initial briefing of the designer right through to the book's publication, the various contributions must remain focused and relevant. Only in this environment can good work ever stand a chance. Too often ideas are diluted because people are scared to stick their necks out, opting instead for a safer, "proven" aesthetic. I very much enjoy employing abstraction and symbolism in my work. I believe it to be much more engaging for the reader when a design merely hints at the book's contents and allows them to fill in the blanks. If your work can activate the reader's interpretive participation, you will make the whole experience more meaningful.

**What are the best and worst things about designing books?**
The best thing is receiving the initial brief, that moment where the possibilities are endless. In short, the time preceding the worst thing ... the moment when you learn that your ideas were not quite what they imagined.

**How would you design a book if there were no limit to budget?**
In many ways there are no limits to what can be achieved with modern-day book design. Production techniques are now very advanced and reasonably priced. The real challenge seems to be choosing to ignore the veritable chocolate-box of finishes and special effects at your disposal. It seems like most books these days aim simply to shout louder than those around them, whereas a well-chosen whisper can often be more effective.

**Do you judge a book by its cover?**
Yes. I almost always buy books on the strength of their jackets, and often solely for the jacket. Books are sold online and in magazines where their covers are shown at less than an inch high, so there is enormous pressure on designers to consider marketing influences as a priority, and to design to target specific markets and readerships. But the biggest challenge for book designers today is to address these issues with confidence and understanding, while still being creative, open-minded, and able to produce the unexpected.

# 05

"I think that the experience of a book
is the same as life—everyone wants
to be seduced."

**Brett Phillips, Australia**

# Extending the Experience

"A book is a complete object that people interact with and keep, and how it looks and feels is a big part of that."

**Jim Stoddart, UK**

# Introduction

Of course, not all books are printed in the same format. This chapter looks at the different and varied formats that a book can take, if the brief allows. The following pages also include examples of books that include added extras for the reader, including stickers, cards, foldouts, and inserts. In some cases these are included for marketing purposes, while in others they form an integral part of the book. In either case they can add value and give the reader a different way in which to interact with the publication.

Design: **Sartoria Comunicazione**
Art Direction: **Sartoria Comunicazione**
Photography: **Duane Michals**
Publisher: **Sartoria Comunicazione/SINV**
Country: **Italy**

## Against My Killer

This book is made up of eight sections, each consisting of eight pages, bound within a solid card cover. The cover is fastened at the spine with a leather tie. This is laced through the front and back pieces and then wrapped around the entire book.

The outer page of each section contains an image from the Against My Killer photo story from Andrew MacKenzie's Fall–Winter 2006/2007 prêt-à-porter and denim haute couture collection. The images are accompanied by hand-written comments from Michals which run through the book, giving it the form of a movie storyboard.

The handwritten text on the cover was applied with a hot foil stamp, and throughout, a screen-print varnish was applied to the photographs. A limited run of 1,001 copies was produced.

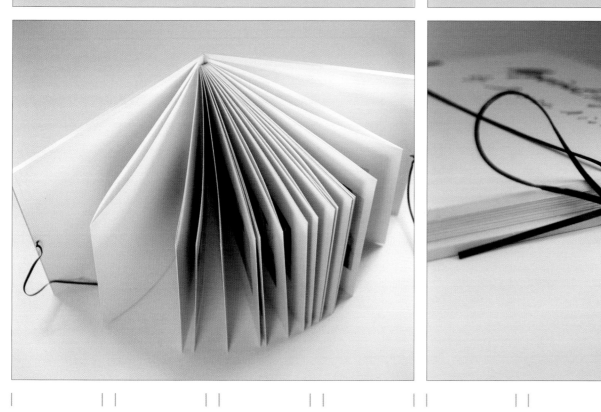

Design: **Airside**
Art Direction: **Airside**
Illustration: **Airside**
Publisher: **Think Tank Media**
Country: **UK**

## Think Tank

This book was designed to promote print-based company Think Tank Media. The brief was to show how the design process works intrinsically with print and packaging, and the various effects that can be produced by printing on different boards and substrates. A number of materials were used to show potential clients how they could print the same finishes on different stocks. The book has a great tactile aspect, and a set of interchangeable cards, each printed on a different surface—from carpet, through velour, to Perspex—has been included. This enables people to engage with the samples straight away. The cover was cloth-bound and embossed with the company's Tony Toad on the back. The company's corporate brown was used for the cover, and its corporate typeface.

Design: **Diesel/Vasava**
Art Direction: **Diesel**
Publisher: **Die Gestalten Verlag**
Countries: **Germany/Italy**

# Fifty

This book, a commemoration of the 50th birthday of Diesel's visionary founder Renzo Rosso, also provides an insight into Diesel's 360° approach to communication. It covers Diesel's key historical moments, products, and special projects, in detail. Through a series of interviews, Rosso shares his personal vision and talks about his life, work, and passions.

With no expense spared, <u>Fifty</u> is full of interactive elements—pop-ups, pullouts, areas to scratch away to reveal secrets, etc. It also comes with a DVD that contains all of Diesel's TV and cinema ads, along with behind-the-scenes footage of Diesel's Talent Supports projects.

The book is covered with different layers; it is like opening a gift. Nestled inside a golden cardboard box is a black PVC slipcase embossed with a gold Fifty ambigram (a logo that can be read right-way round or upside down), inside which is the actual book. The title has been applied using glossy UV varnish on the soft, white flock cover.

In keeping with the eclectic nature of Diesel's projects, and the contents of the book, a wide range of fonts has been used. These include a modified Avant Garde for the chapter headlines, Miller for the main text, and Eagle for the introductory text.

Design: **Adriana Deléo-Stubbe/Wyeth Hansen/Joe Marianek/Ryan Waller/ Lily Williams**
Publisher: **Rhode Island School of Design**
Country: **USA**

## RISD Yearbook 2003

This is the 2003 yearbook for graduating students of the Rhode Island School of Design. "The RISD yearbooks had traditionally been conceptual and highbrow, departing from the book form, such as a roll of toilet paper or box of photos," explains Marianek. "Year to year, the organizational principle had been to let each student create their own 'exhibition' page or space featuring their work, but firstly, the majority of students didn't participate because they were too busy to submit work, and secondly, the 'one page for each student' model did not accurately capture the spirit of the work."

Marianek and his fellow graduates decided to make a "fun artifact that could have an ongoing dynamic use" as well as bring it back to a book form that would be immediately nostalgic. It follows traditional book form, with a half title, colophon, etc, and all the traditional parts of the book were designed to look unembellished and institutional, to counteract with the fun stickers that featured images of the students as well as short texts. To complete the package, the dark brown, faux leather, hardbound book was wrapped in a jacket that looks like a candy-bar wrapper.

Serif and sans-serif typefaces were used throughout—Malmo Sans (for its humble and quiet nature) to set people's names, and Lubalin Graph (with its dated and nostalgic look) for titling and institutional text. The book's grid was designed to fit in around 600 student photos.

Design: **Matthias Ernstberger** at
    **Sagmeister Inc.**
Art Direction: **Stefan Sagmeister**
Typography: **Marian Bantjes**
Production: **Lara Fieldbinder/**
    **Melissa Secundino**
Publisher: **Deutsche Guggenheim**
Country: **USA**

## Douglas Gordon's
## The Vanity of Allegory

This postcard-book box set was created
around Douglas Gordon's exhibition
"The Vanity of Allegory," which was held
at the Deutsche Guggenheim in Berlin.
Inspired by the title of the exhibition,
the designers have created a cover that
incorporates the clever use of a slanted
mirror. Together with typography by
Bantjes, the mirror is used to create the
word "vanity." The box was silk-screen
printed on black 400gsm board and
folded to incorporate a mirror plate,
which was applied by hand.

The postcards are printed in five colors
on 330gsm cover stock.

Design: **Nikolaj Knop and Martin Fredricson at WE RECOMMEND**
Art Direction: **WE RECOMMEND**
Publisher: **Fivestarday**
Country: **Sweden**

## Action Spaces

Malmö-based Fivestarday produces strategic web solutions. "Fivestarday wanted a book that explained the concept of action spaces and expressed the company's alternative attitude toward web development," explain Knop and Fredricson. Action Spaces describes Fivestarday's way of working with IT strategy. The book and company identity is based on a pattern that symbolizes both Fivestarday's name and working method. In the spaces between the pattern's elements, five stars appear. The pattern is built on a grid that enables all the elements to be put together in an indefinite number of ways. Thus the pattern never appears the same twice.

Clarendon typeface has been used throughout. The book has been bound with glue to allow it to be opened flat. It comes with a paper pad to encourage users to sketch their own action grid.

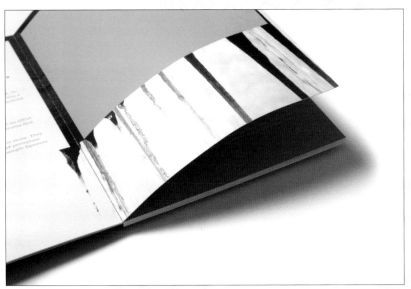

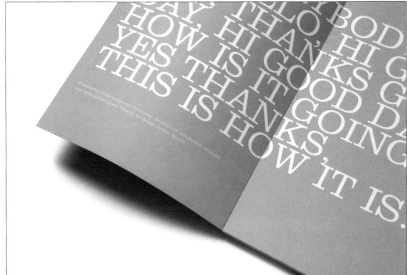

ACTION SPACE
ATTITUDE
+
ACTION SPACE GRID
=
ACTION SPACE

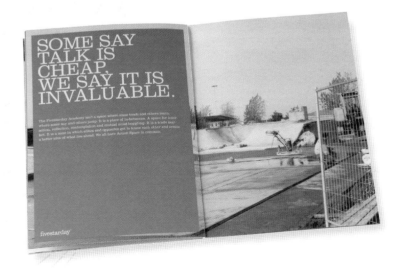

Design: **Roanne Adams**
Art Direction: **Surface to Air**
Publisher: **Surface to Air**
Countries: **USA/Japan**

## Flip the Script

Recognizing the intrinsic effect that cinema has had on the art world, Surface to Air commissioned 50 artists to recreate, reinterpret, reinvent, reshape, and remix a poster for a movie of their choice. The results were printed in this poster-sized book, <u>Flip the Script</u>.

The concept behind the design was to showcase the artwork created by the various artists, photographers, and designers as movie posters, which, if desired, could be removed from the book. "The idea was to design it simply and cleanly, but evoke the feeling of cinema," explains Adams. "The book also aims to present the work in a format which reflects the grandiose influence and scope of cinema, along with its tradition of posters."

Red canvas was used on the cover together with a fake leather bind, and the title applied in a gold emboss.

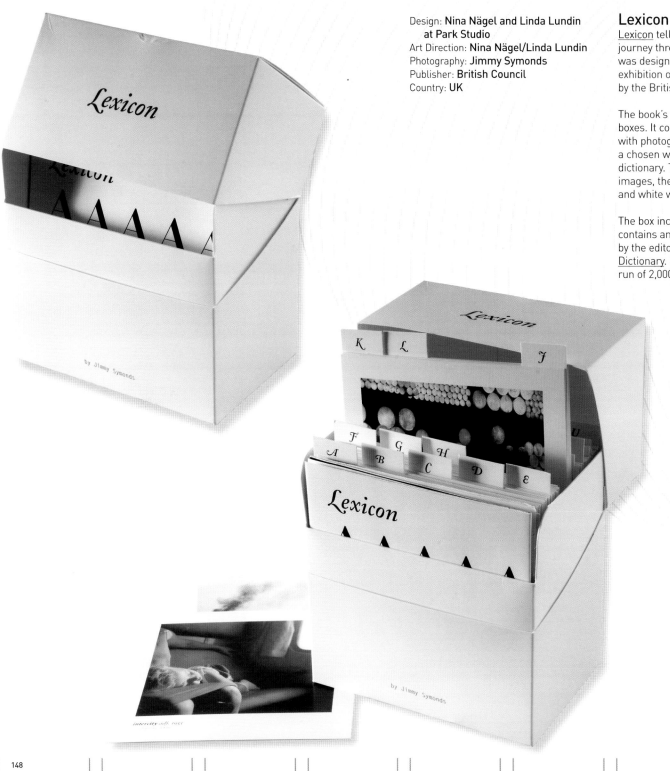

Design: **Nina Nägel and Linda Lundin at Park Studio**
Art Direction: **Nina Nägel/Linda Lundin**
Photography: **Jimmy Symonds**
Publisher: **British Council**
Country: **UK**

## Lexicon

Lexicon tells the story of Symonds' journey through a dictionary. This book was designed to accompany the traveling exhibition of the same name, sponsored by the British Council.

The book's format was inspired by index boxes. It contains 144 removable cards with photographs, each one illustrating a chosen word or phrase from the dictionary. To echo the monochrome images, the designers used only black and white within the design.

The box includes a folded poster that contains an introductory essay written by the editors of the Oxford English Dictionary. It was produced in a limited run of 2,000.

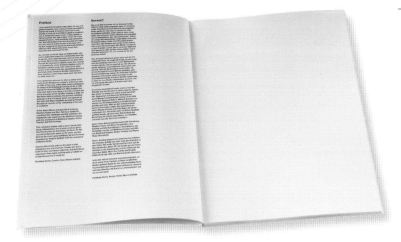

Design: **William Hall/Dennis Hankvist**
Art Direction: **William Hall**
Photography: **Hélène Binet**
Publisher: **Henry Moore Publications**
Country: **UK**

## Imi Knoebel: Primary Structures 1966/2006

This book was created to accompany an exhibition of Imi Knoebel's work. Displaying early and recent works, it examined the relationship between sculpture and painting, demonstrating not only the constructed quality of painting, but also the links between installation and painting. The large format was a response to the scale of Knoebel's work.

"We divided text and images so that they are never juxtaposed," explains Hall. "Left-hand pages have text, right-hand pages have images. We did this partly so that you could read the images alone as a visual essay." The book was litho printed and flexibound.

Design: **Christian Hundertmark at C100**
Art Direction: **Christian Hundertmark**
Publisher: **Publikat Verlags und Handels**
Country: **Germany**

# The Art of Rebellion 1/
# The Art of Rebellion 2

The Art of Rebellion (AOR) books focus on the phenomenon of street art and urban art activism around the world. They feature interviews with the artists and reports from various cities.

Hundertmark, with his background in graffiti, came up with the concept for the books. "After years of being more active in graphic design and illustration, street art was like a rebirth for my feelings toward urban art," he explains. "At the time that I did AOR 1 there were no books available for this young movement, so I came up with the idea of bringing out a book about it both from the artist's and the graphic designer's side."

For the image used on the cover of AOR 1, Hundertmark photographed a lamppost and then created a sticker banderole that featured the work of the various different artists in the book. This enabled the reader to choose which stickers to put on the lamppost to create their own cover. For AOR 2, Hundertmark created a fist image using the various featured artists' street logos.

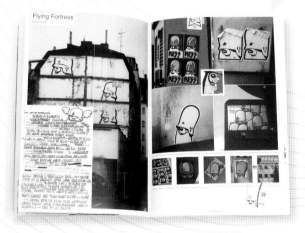

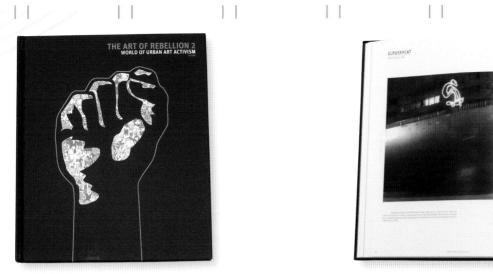

EXTENDING THE EXPERIENCE

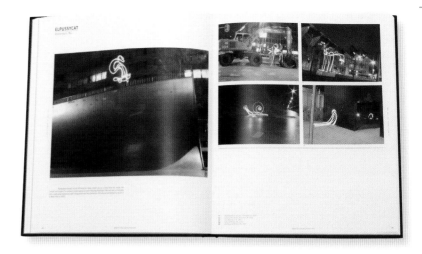

**ELPUSSYCAT**

**DAVE THE CHIMP**
London, UK

**KLISTERPETE**
Stockholm, SE

## Nick Bell, Nick Bell Design, UK

**What and when was the first book you designed?**
I designed numerous book covers in the late 1980s, but not a whole book until 2000. It was a Mona Hatoum catalog for Tate Britain called The Entire World as a Foreign Land, which was only 44 pages. I've always considered Eye more a book than a magazine, so perhaps that was my first, in 1997. I designed 31 of them over an eight-year period.

**What is your favorite book cover/overall package design?**
Karel Martens: printed matter\drukwerk. I have a special edition with a white cover that Karel gave me personally. It is a scrapbook of controlled chaos and as physically unpretentious as they come—unlike most books, which tend to elevate their content too much. I keep PTT Telecom phone cards designed by Karel, and featured in the book, in the folds of its cover.

**What makes a good book cover?**
One that distills its content in a memorable way.

**How much of a role do you think the designer plays as a marketer in the retail environment?**
We have far too little say. Often the book designer will be prevented from designing the cover. Besides, covers have limited influence now that so many books are bought online. A good set of book reviews is probably much more important.

**What are the best and worst things about designing books?**
The best is having the time to do a good job, as most books run on generous lead times. That's my experience anyway. The worst is not having enough time, but at least you stand a chance of making some money if it's done fast.

**How would you design a book if there were no limit to budget?**
I would set one and put the rest of the money to work on something more ecologically responsible.

**Do you judge a book by its cover?**
No, because too many good books are let down by poor covers.

## Jim Stoddart, Penguin Books, UK

**What and when was the first book you designed?**
On The Road by Jack Kerouac for the Penguin Modern Classic relaunch in 2000.

**When approaching book design, what inspires you?**
Anything and everything. The spirit of the books themselves, but also music, art, movies, history, attitudes, cultural trends, architecture, etc.

**What makes a good book cover?**
A unique, succinct, and iconic solution that you just have to have.

**How much of a role do you think the designer plays as a marketer in the retail environment?**
As most books do not have a marketing budget, the cover is essentially 100 percent of a book's initial marketing pull in a store. The front of the book is like a little poster that either makes someone pick it up or walk past it. Only once a book has been picked up is the book itself able to draw a potential reader in further. However, the way most online book sites are currently set up, covers play a much less significant role, and I find myself going straight to the customer reviews.

**What are the best and worst things about designing books?**
The best thing is trying to sum up 300 pages of writing in one small design. The scope for creativity is huge and it's a different solution every time. The worst thing is the occasional politics involved and ending up with an uninspired, and uninspiring, design by committee.

**How would you design a book if there were no limit to budget?**
In the world of popular publishing, and particularly paperback publishing, having a large budget doesn't necessarily affect the way a book is designed. If you have a great cover design for a paperback, then it might only need to be printed on the simplest of boards to have a beautiful charm and integrity.

**Do you judge a book by its cover?**
Definitely. A piece of writing deserves to be read on its own merits, but a book is a complete object that people interact with and keep, and how it looks and feels is a big part of that.

# Contact Details & Acknowledgments

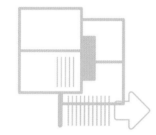

# Contact Details

**3 Deep Design**
www.3deep.com.au / design@3deep.com.au

**Airside**
www.airside.co.uk / studio@airside.co.uk

**Aufuldish & Warinner**
www.aufwar.com / bob@aufwar.com

**Base**
www.basedesign.com / basenyc@basedesign.com

**Big Active**
www.bigactive.com

**Bleed**
www.bleed.com / bleed@bleed.no

**Bluemark Inc.**
www.bluemark.co.jp / info@bluemark.co.jp

**Browns**
www.brownsdesign.com / info@brownsdesign.com

**BuroLamp**
www.burolamp.com

**C100**
www.c100studio.com / hello@c100studio.com

**Deanne Cheuk Design**
www.deannecheuk.com / neomuworld@aol.com

**The Consult**
www.theconsult.com / info@theconsult.com

**Die Gestalten Verlag**
www.die-gestalten.de

**Paulus M. Dreibholz**
www.dreibholz.com / studio@dreibholz.com

**Eat Sleep Work/Play**
www.eatsleepworkplay.co.uk

**Eggers + Diaper**
www.eggers-diaper.com

**Jonathan Ellery**
www.jonathanellery.com

**Faber Design**
www.faber.co.uk / darrenw@faber.co.uk

**FriendsWithYou**
www.friendswithyou.com

**Frost Design**
www.frostdesign.com.au / vince.frost@frostdesign.com.au

**Gabor Palotai Design**
www.gaborpalotai.com / design@gaborpalotai.com

**Birna Geirfinnsdóttir**
www.birnageirfinns.com / birna@birnageirfinns.com

**General Working Group**
www.generalworkinggroup.com /
geoff@ generalworkinggroup.com.com

**Rob Giesendorf**
www.robgiesendorf.nl / robgiesendorf@gmail.com

**Joost Grootens**
www.grootens.nl / joost@grootens.nl

**William Hall**
www.williamhall.co.uk

**Wyeth Hansen**
www.wyethhansen.com

**Daphne Heemskerk**
www.daphneheemskerk.com /
info@daphneheemskerk.com

**Hesign Publishing**
www.hesign.com / info@hesign.com

**Sól Hrafnsdóttir**
www.grafiksense.net / sol@grafiksense.net

**i.o.u.**
www.eyeohhewe.co.uk / ste@eyeohhewe.co.uk

**Is Not Magazine**
www.isnotmagazine.org / info@isnotmagazine.org

**karlssonwilker inc.**
www.karlssonwilker.com /
tellmewhy@karlssonwilker.com

**Kelly Verhallen Graphic Design**
www.kellyverhallen.com / kellyverhallen@hotmail.com

**Kerr | Noble**
www.kerrnoble.com / info@kerrnoble.com

Rafael Koch
r.koch@gmx.ch

Lotta Kühlhorn
www.lottakuhlhorn.se / lotta@kuhlhorn.se

David Lane
www.davidlaneuk.net / dave@davidlaneuk.net

Joe Marianek
www.joemarianek.com

Hörður Lárusson
www.larusson.com / hordur@larusson.com

Marcelo Mendiguebel
www.rdya.com / info@rdya.com.ar

Martin Mischkulnig
www.martinmischkulnig.com

Meike Kersholt
www.meikster.nl / meike.kersholt@gmail.com

Mues Design
www.muesdesign.com / Melanie@muesdesign.com

Nick Bell Design
www.nickbelldesign.co.uk / studio@nickbelldesign.co.uk

No Days Off
www.nodaysoff.com / info@nodaysoff.com

Park Studio
www.park-studio.com / park@park-studio.com

David Pearson
www.davidpearsondesign.com / info@davidpearsondesign.com

Pentagram
www.pentagram.com

Peter and Paul
www.peterandpaul.co.uk / paul@peterandpaul.co.uk

Ricardo Drab y Asociados
www.rdya.com / info@rdya.com.ar

Rinzen
www.rinzen.com / they@rinzen.com

Roanne Adams Design
www.roanneadams.com / ro@roanneadams.com

Chris Rubino
www.chrisrubino.com / crubino@studio18hundred.com

Sagmeister Inc.
www.sagmeister.com / info@sagmeister.com

Sartoria Comunicazione
www.sartoria.com / info@sartoria.com

SEA Design
www.seadesign.co.uk

Clare Skeats
www.clareskeats.co.uk / clare@clareskeats.co.uk

Sopp Collective
www.soppcollective.com / contact@soppcollective.com

Spin
www.spin.co.uk / patricia@spin.co.uk

Stripe LA
www.stripela.com / gail@stripela.com

Surface
www.surface.de / info@surface.de

Surface to Air
www.surface2air.com / nyc@surface2air.com

Underware
www.underware.nl

Undoboy
www.undoboy.com / contact@undoboy.com

Ryan Waller
www.thingmaking.com / ryan@thingmaking.com

WE RECOMMEND
www.werecommend.se / mail@werecommend.se

Lily Williams
www.my-name-is.com / lily_williams@mac.com

# Acknowledgments

Many thanks to all the designers, art directors, and publishers around the world who, through their contributions, have made this book possible. Special thanks also to Brett Phillips, Jiaping He, Jonathan Ellery, Darren Wall, Joe Marianek, David Pearson, Nick Bell, and Jim Stoddart. Thanks to Simon Punter for his photography, Simon Slater for his design, and finally, thanks to the team at RotoVision.

This book is for Mum.

# Index